Funny Short Stories for Seniors

A Collection of Easy-to-Read, Brain-Stimulating Stories for Seniors Living with Dementia

Martin Miller

TEXT COPYRIGHT © Martin Miller

All rights reserved. No part of this guide may be reproduced in any form without permission in writing from the publisher except in the case of brief quotations embodied in critical articles or reviews.

LEGAL & DISCLAIMER

The information contained in this book and its contents is not designed to replace or take the place of any form of medical or professional advice; and is not meant to replace the need for independent medical, financial, legal, or other professional advice or services, as may be required. The content and information in this book has been provided for educational and entertainment purposes only.

The content and information contained in this book has been compiled from sources deemed reliable, and it is accurate to the best of the Author's knowledge, information, and belief. However, the Author cannot guarantee its accuracy and validity and cannot be held liable for any errors and/or omissions. Further, changes are periodically made to this book as and when needed. Where appropriate and/or necessary, you must consult a professional (including but not limited to your doctor, attorney, financial advisor, or such other professional advisor) before using any of the suggested remedies, techniques, or information in this book.

Upon using the contents and information contained in this book, you agree to hold harmless the Author from and against any damages, costs, and expenses, including any legal fees potentially resulting from the application of any of the information provided by this book. This disclaimer applies to any loss, damages or injury caused by the use and application, whether directly or indirectly, of any advice or information presented, whether for breach of contract, tort, negligence, personal injury, criminal intent, or under any other cause of action. You agree to accept all risks of using the information presented inside this book.

You agree that by continuing to read this book, where appropriate and/or necessary, you shall consult a professional (including but not limited to your doctor, attorney, or financial advisor or such other advisor as needed) before using any of the suggested remedies, techniques, or information in this book.

TABLE OF CONTENT

INTRODUCTION — 5

Lost in Distractions: A Shopping Tale — 6
The Elusive Sock Safari — 8
The Hilarious Adventures of Old Friends — 10
The Crossword Conundrum Club — 12
The Late-Blooming Comedian — 14
The Mischievous Grandpas: Prank Wars — 16
Sun-Kissed Lesson — 18
The Whimsical Adventures of Grandpa and Grandson — 20
The Dress Surprise — 22
The Dream Court: A Playful Journey to Justice — 24
The Case of the Ticklish Feather — 26
The Great Quest for Grandma's Glasses — 28
The Remote Control Mischief — 30
The Great Caper — 32
The Pillow Prank — 34
The Tickling Troupe — 36
The Topsy-Turvy Recipe: A Hilarious Culinary Adventure — 38
The Elusive Walking Cane — 40
The Hidden Treasures: Grandma's Mischief — 42
The Joyful Recipe Adventurer — 44
The Whistling Teapot — 46
The Football Rivalry of Grandpa Joe and Grandpa Frank — 48
Grandpa's Golfing Adventure — 50
The Unforgettable Surprise — 52

Clara's Courageous Flight	54
The Melodies of Remembrance	56
The Adventures of Mr. Thompson	58
The Mismatched Sock Tradition	60
The Mischievous Umbrella	62
Grandma and Granddaughter's Delightful Adventures	64
The Suit Mismatch: A Hilarious Fashion Adventure	66
The Unforgettable Picnic: A Tale of Mismatched Tastes	68
The Mysterious Adventures of Granny Edna	70
The Nutty Surprise: Grandma's Delicious Discovery	72
Brushes of Dreams: Embracing Passion at Any Age	74
Clara and the Mysterious Corn Disappearance	76
The Laughter Within: Embracing Life's Whimsy with Henry	78
A Slice of Laughter: The Apple Pie Adventure	80
The Joyful Game with a Furry Friend	82
The Magical Painting Adventure	84
The Timeless Dream	86
The Pancake Mishap: A Recipe for Laughter	88
The Grandson's Mischievous Scare	90
The Unforgettable Dance	92
The Hilarious Fishing Expedition	94
From Skeptic to Savory: Grandpa's Journey to Healthy Eating	96
The Whistling Teapot	98
The Mysterious Case of the Vanishing Cookies	100
The Gift of a Second Chance	102
Grandma's Hilarious Yoga Journey	104
The Mischievous Legacy of Harold's Rubber Chicken Prank	106
The Hilarious Misadventures of Grandpa and Grandson	108

The Yarn-Filled Shenanigans	110
The Forgetful Reminder	112
The Mischievous Duo at the Senior Home	114
The Courageous Chicken	116
Grandpa Friends: Fishing Adventure	118
The Adventurous Grannies: A Joyful Journey	120
Blooming Memories: Grandma and Granddaughter's Floral Journey	122
The Mischievous Dentures	124
The Whistle-Blowing Concert	126
The Forgiving Grandma	128
The Hilarious Hide-and-Seek with Hank the Hound	130
The Mischievous Parrot and the Stolen Breakfast	132
The Whimsical Hat Collection	134
The Forgetful Duo	136
The Grand Pajama Party Revival	138
Grandpa's Zoo Adventure	140
The Elusive Slipper: A Hilarious Quest for the Perfect Fit	142
Tea and Masquerade: A Delightful Tradition	144
Grandma's Tales: A Timeless Connection	146
The Jolly Jest Fest	148
Grandpa Chef: A Flavorful Tale	150
The Silver Squad's Spectacular Scavenger Hunt	152
Dancing Duo: Laughter Unleashed	154
CONCLUSION	155

INTRODUCTION

With excitement and joy, I present to you this wonderful book filled with funny and inspiring stories about old folks, love, and laughter. Within its pages, you will find lighthearted narratives that will make you smile, laugh, and perhaps even shed a tear of joy.

These stories are the product of imagination and inspiration, but at their core, they embody true values and emotions that accompany us throughout our lives. They speak of wisdom, friendship, adventures, and a positive outlook that can accompany us even in our golden years.

From an old man who rediscovers humor and playfulness to a grandmother who experiences the joy of a pajama party once again, these stories invite you to embrace the spirit of boundless optimism and realize that meaning and happiness can be found at any age.

Prepare to be swept up in the humorous escapades of these extraordinary individuals. Laugh along as they navigate the challenges of technology, embark on unexpected adventures, and find new passions and friendships along the way. Through their laughter and resilience, they teach us valuable lessons about embracing change, cherishing relationships, and embracing the joy of each passing moment.

Each page of this book welcomes you into a world of smiles, laughter, and warmth, reminding us of the importance of our loved ones, friendship, and never ceasing to dream and enjoy life.

Let these stories be a source of inspiration, motivation, and fun in your life. May they remind you that age is irrelevant when you have love, humor, and a desire to share joy with others.

So, sit back, relax, and allow yourself to be immersed in the captivating world of «Aging with Laughter: Heartwarming Stories of Old Folks.» Let their laughter fill your heart and remind you that the golden years are truly a time for embracing life's extraordinary moments.

Happy reading!

Lost in Distractions: A Shopping Tale

Once upon a time, there was a man named Henry who embarked on a simple mission to buy some powder from the store. Henry was known for being easily distracted and often found himself getting sidetracked by various things that caught his attention.

On this particular day, Henry entered the store with a clear purpose in mind—to buy powder. He confidently made his way down the aisles, but as he passed through each section, he couldn't help but get lured by other items.

First, he noticed a display of colorful socks that caught his eye. He thought to himself, «Well, I could use some new socks.» So he picked up a few pairs and added them to his cart.

As he continued his journey, Henry stumbled upon a shelf filled with books. Being an avid reader, he couldn't resist the temptation. He browsed through the titles, engrossed in the world of possibilities. Before he knew it, his cart was now filled with a stack of books.

Next, Henry found himself in the snack aisle. The array of delicious treats beckoned him, and he couldn't resist grabbing a bag of his favorite chips and some chocolate bars. They seemed like the perfect companions for his reading adventures.

Finally, after meandering through various aisles, Henry realized he had strayed far from his original mission—to buy powder.

He chuckled to himself, realizing how easily he had become distracted. With a grin on his face, Henry headed to the checkout counter, where he unloaded his cart filled with socks, books, and snacks. The cashier couldn't help but laugh at the sight of it all.

As Henry left the store, he couldn't help but feel a sense of amusement. Although he hadn't achieved his initial goal of buying powder, he had unintentionally filled his cart with items that brought him joy and excitement.

Henry's adventure at the store taught him a valuable lesson about embracing life's detours and finding delight in the unexpected. He realized that sometimes, the most memorable experiences come from deviating from our plans and following the whims of curiosity.

From that day forward, whenever Henry went shopping, he made a conscious effort to remain open to the surprises that awaited him. And although he occasionally forgot to buy the things he originally intended, he found that the journey itself was often more rewarding than the destination.

So, if you ever spot Henry at the store, don't be surprised if he's enthusiastically exploring the aisles, his cart filled with a mix of unexpected treasures, and a smile on his face. For he has learned that sometimes, it's the detours that lead to the greatest adventures.

The Elusive Sock Safari

Have you ever lost anything? Well, let me tell you a rib-tickling tale about Grandpa's epic sock search.

One sunny morning, Grandpa woke up with a spring in his step, ready to conquer the day. He cheerfully put on his slippers and set out to find his favorite pair of cozy socks. But to his surprise, one sock seemed to have vanished into thin air!

Undeterred by the mystery, Grandpa embarked on a sock safari throughout his house. He searched under the bed, behind the couch, and even inside the cookie jar (because, well, you never know where socks might wander off to). But alas, the missing sock remained elusive.

With determination in his eyes and a magnifying glass in hand, Grandpa scoured every nook and cranny. He peeked into drawers, checked under the kitchen sink, and even enlisted the help of his faithful cat, Whiskers, who was equally perplexed by the sock's disappearance.

Hours turned into a whole day, and Grandpa's sock search had become a family affair. His grandchildren joined the mission, crawling on the floor, and peeking into unlikely hiding spots, giggling all the while.

As the sun began to set, and hope started to wane, Grandpa sat down on his favorite armchair, feeling defeated. He gazed at his feet, thinking about the lost sock and the curious places it could have wandered off to.

But as he lowered his gaze, a sudden burst of laughter erupted from the room. Everyone's eyes were fixed on Grandpa's feet, and there it was—the missing sock, snugly tucked between his slippers, right where he had left it!

Grandpa's face turned beet red as he realized the irony of his grand sock search. The whole day's adventure had revolved around a sock that had never left his side.

Amidst a chorus of laughter, Grandpa joined in on the mirth, shaking his head at the silliness of it all. The family couldn't stop teasing him, playfully reminding him to check his slippers first next time.

From that day forward, whenever someone in the family couldn't find something, they would jokingly say, «Maybe it's just playing hide-and-seek like Grandpa's sock!»

And so, the tale of Grandpa's elusive sock became a legend, bringing laughter and joy to family gatherings for years to come. It served as a gentle reminder that sometimes, the things we search for are closer than we think, and that laughter is the best companion on any quest, no matter how small.

The Hilarious Adventures of Old Friends

Once upon a time, in a cozy little town, two lifelong friends, Agnes and Mildred, set out on an unforgettable escapade.

One sunny afternoon, Agnes and Mildred decided to explore a newly opened amusement park in their town. Armed with their senior citizen discount tickets and an uncontainable excitement, they embarked on their adventure.

Their first stop was the roller coaster, a towering beast that twisted and turned with exhilarating speed. As they waited in line, Agnes turned to Mildred with a mischievous grin and said, «Mildred, are we too old for this?»

Mildred winked and replied, «Oh, Agnes, we're never too old for a thrill!»

With that, they boarded the roller coaster, holding onto each other tightly as the ride took off. Their screams of excitement echoed throughout the park, and people couldn't help but laugh at the sight of two spirited old friends experiencing the ride of their lives.

Next, Agnes and Mildred decided to test their aim at the water gun game. Determined to win a prize, they each picked up a water gun and took aim at the target. However, their water guns seemed to have a mind of their own, squirting water in all directions except at the target.

Laughing uncontrollably, they soaked themselves and everyone around them, creating a delightful water spectacle that left everyone drenched and smiling.

As the day wore on, Agnes and Mildred tried their luck at various attractions – from the Ferris wheel, where they shouted words of encouragement to each other from the highest point, to the bumper cars, where they bumped into every other car except each other's.

Their laughter became infectious, spreading throughout the amusement park and drawing curious onlookers. People couldn't help but join in the merriment, inspired by the genuine joy radiating from these two vivacious old friends.

As the sun began to set, Agnes and Mildred sat on a bench, catching their breath and relishing in the memories they had created that day. They shared stories of their past adventures and laughed until tears streamed down their cheeks.

In that moment, surrounded by the twinkling lights of the amusement park, Agnes and Mildred realized that age was merely a number. Their friendship and zest for life were timeless, reminding them that no matter how old they grew, their spirit would forever remain young at heart.

With a final burst of energy, Agnes and Mildred joined hands and danced to the sound of music playing in the distance, twirling and spinning like carefree teenagers.

And so, the hilarious adventures of Agnes and Mildred became legendary in their town, reminding everyone that laughter, friendship, and a childlike spirit could make even the simplest moments unforgettable.

The Crossword Conundrum Club

In the bustling common room of a senior care facility, a group of spirited individuals gathered every afternoon. Among them was a remarkable assembly of crossword enthusiasts, each grappling with the challenges of dementia. But within the walls of their crossword haven, they found solace, camaraderie, and a collective determination to unravel the mysteries of language.

Led by their vivacious coordinator, Emma, the group embarked on a daily quest to conquer crossword puzzles of varying degrees of complexity. As they huddled around the table, pencils poised and minds primed for discovery, the room buzzed with anticipation.

With each clue presented, their memories danced on the tip of their tongues. Some words remained elusive, drifting through the corridors of their minds. But their collective strength, fueled by friendship, transformed these moments of forgetfulness into opportunities for collaboration.

Harry, the retired librarian, would share snippets of literary knowledge, sparking inspiration and triggering forgotten words. Elizabeth, a former history teacher, would offer historical context, weaving tales that sparked connections. And Sarah, a retired scientist, would approach clues with a logical mindset, piecing together answers like a puzzle within a puzzle.

Their sessions became a delightful blend of laughter, creative thinking, and gentle nudges of remembrance.

With every solved crossword, they celebrated not just the victory of completing a puzzle, but also the resilience and triumph of the human spirit.

As the days turned into weeks and weeks into months, the Crossword Conundrum Club grew in popularity. Residents from other wings of the care facility eagerly joined the group, bringing their own unique perspectives and experiences to the table. The power of collective wisdom and shared camaraderie transformed the club into a vibrant community, where everyone found solace and purpose.

Outside the confines of their crossword haven, members of the club discovered newfound confidence. They carried their love for words into everyday conversations, weaving anecdotes and clever phrases that sparked smiles in the hearts of those around them.

The Crossword Conundrum Club not only provided intellectual stimulation but also nourished their spirits. In a world where memories were elusive, the camaraderie and shared accomplishments became touchstones of joy, reminding each member that they were more than their individual challenges.

Their story spread beyond the walls of the care facility, inspiring others to embrace the power of connection and the resilience of the human mind. The Crossword Conundrum Club became a testament to the enduring strength of the human spirit, proving that even in the face of forgetfulness, the pursuit of knowledge and the bonds of friendship could light the way to brighter tomorrows.

The Late-Blooming Comedian

Have you ever had a secret dream that seemed too big to chase? Meet Grandpa Frank, a kind-hearted gentleman who had harbored a lifelong dream of becoming a comedian. But there was one thing holding him back – shyness.

For years, Grandpa Frank kept his comedic aspirations tucked away, hidden behind a reserved smile. He believed that his desire to make people laugh was better left unsaid. That was until he found himself living in a retirement home surrounded by new friends who craved laughter and joy.

One Thursday afternoon, during a casual gathering with his fellow residents, Grandpa Frank summoned the courage to share a funny story. He mustered all his wit, gathered his nerves, and began recounting a hilarious tale from his youth. To his surprise, his friends burst into laughter, their eyes twinkling with delight.

Encouraged by their response, Grandpa Frank embraced his newfound role as the resident comedian. Every Thursday, he would eagerly prepare a collection of life's humorous anecdotes, carefully selecting the perfect jokes to share with his beloved audience. The retirement home became his comedy club, and his friends, his biggest fans.

As the weeks went by, Grandpa Frank's comedic talent grew. He learned to read his audience, tailoring his jokes to their unique personalities.

His performances became the highlight of the week, filling the room with infectious laughter and creating a sense of camaraderie among the residents.

Word of Grandpa Frank's comedic prowess spread beyond the retirement home. Soon, he found himself invited to perform at local community centers, charity events, and even nearby schools. His zest for life and ability to find humor in the simplest of things resonated with people of all ages.

The once-shy Grandpa Frank had blossomed into a confident and beloved comedian, bringing joy to the lives of those around him. His dream had finally come true, and he realized that it's never too late to pursue what sets your soul on fire.

Grandpa Frank's journey taught everyone a valuable lesson – that life is meant to be embraced, cherished, and celebrated, even in the golden years. His laughter-filled performances became a source of inspiration, reminding everyone that dreams are not limited by age or circumstance.

So, if you find yourself with a secret dream hidden away, remember Grandpa Frank's story. Let his late-blooming journey be a testament to the fact that it's never too late to chase your dreams, share your talents, and spread laughter wherever you go.

The Mischievous Grandpas: Prank Wars

Once upon a time, in a quiet little town, there were two mischievous grandpas named Henry and Walter. They had been friends since childhood and loved playing pranks on each other. Every day was an opportunity for them to come up with clever schemes and jokes.

One sunny afternoon, Grandpa Henry came up with a brilliant idea. He decided to hide a whoopee cushion on Grandpa Walter's favorite armchair. He couldn't wait to see Walter's reaction when he sat down and heard the funny sound. With a mischievous grin, Henry carefully placed the cushion and waited for the perfect moment.

Later that day, as Walter sat down on his armchair, a loud «Pfffft!» echoed through the room. He jumped up in surprise, his face turning bright red. Realizing he had fallen victim to Henry's prank, he burst into laughter.

But Grandpa Walter wasn't one to back down easily. He was determined to get back at Henry with an even better prank. The next day, Walter snuck into Henry's workshop and filled his toolbox with fake spiders. He couldn't help but giggle at the thought of Henry's reaction.

When Henry went to grab a tool from his toolbox, he let out a yelp and jumped back in fright. The sight of the fake spiders made his heart race for a moment, but then he burst into laughter, realizing Walter had outdone himself.

And so, the prank wars between Henry and Walter continued. They hid whoopee cushions, swapped sugar with salt, and even replaced toothpaste with mayonnaise. Their mischievous antics brought joy and laughter not only to each other but to the entire town.

Their pranks became legendary, and people eagerly awaited the next trick they would play on each other. But amidst all the laughter and jokes, their friendship remained strong. They knew how to push each other's buttons, but they also knew how to support and uplift one another.

As the years passed, Henry and Walter became the town's beloved pranksters. They taught everyone that laughter was the best medicine, no matter how old you were. Their friendship served as a reminder that age is just a number and that mischievous spirits can bring endless joy.

So, if you ever find yourself in a small town, be on the lookout for two mischievous grandpas named Henry and Walter. They might just brighten your day with a clever prank and remind you that life is meant to be enjoyed with a good dose of humor.

Sun-Kissed Lesson

Have you ever had a moment when you thought you had everything under control, only to realize that you missed an important detail? Well, let me share with you the funny story of Grandma Martha and her beach escapade.

One beautiful summer morning, Grandma Martha decided to treat herself to a day of relaxation by the ocean. Excited about the idea, she called up her best friend, Mary, to invite her along. Mary, being the responsible one, reminded Grandma Martha to bring her sunscreen.

«Martha, don't forget your sunscreen. We don't want you turning into a lobster!» Mary jokingly warned. Grandma Martha assured Mary that she would remember and chuckled at the thought of turning into a lobster. Little did she know, her memory would play a trick on her.

The next day, armed with her beach towel and a good book, Grandma Martha made her way to the sandy shore. As she settled into her beach chair, she couldn't help but notice the vibrant blue sky and the inviting ocean waves. The sun's warm rays kissed her skin, and she basked in the glorious feeling of relaxation.

But as the day wore on, Grandma Martha started to feel a tingling sensation on her skin. She glanced down and gasped – her arms and legs were turning a vibrant shade of red! She had forgotten to apply sunscreen and now had a sunburn to prove it.

Feeling a bit sheepish, Grandma Martha reflected on the importance of being prompt and responsible. She realized that even the smallest tasks, like applying sunscreen, could have a big impact on her well-being.

From that day forward, Grandma Martha made a promise to herself to always stay organized and complete tasks in a timely manner. Whether it was applying sunscreen, paying bills, or simply keeping track of important dates, she understood the value of being proactive and responsible.

As Grandma Martha healed from her sunburn, she couldn't help but smile at the valuable lesson she had learned. The experience served as a reminder that taking care of oneself goes beyond just physical well-being. It meant being attentive, responsible, and mindful of the little things that contribute to a happy and healthy life.

So, the next time you find yourself tempted to procrastinate or forget an important task, remember Grandma Martha and her sunburn adventure. Embrace the lesson she learned and strive to do everything in a timely manner. After all, life is too precious to let forgetfulness stand in the way of enjoying every moment under the sun.

The Whimsical Adventures of Grandpa and Grandson

Once upon a time, in a charming little town, lived an adventurous grandpa named Henry and his curious grandson, Ethan. Their days were filled with laughter, mischief, and a pinch of magic that seemed to follow them wherever they went.

Grandpa Henry was known for his imaginative stories, brimming with tales of daring escapades and mythical creatures. He would whisk Ethan away on grand adventures, embarking on quests to find hidden treasures or unravel ancient mysteries. Together, they would explore the deepest forests, climb towering mountains, and sail across imaginary seas.

But as the years passed, Grandpa Henry's memory started to play tricks on him. He would forget the names of the characters in his stories or mix up their daring feats. It was a challenge that tested their bond, but they refused to let it dim their spirits.

Instead of getting disheartened, Ethan embraced the opportunity to become the hero of their stories. He would nudge Grandpa Henry's memory with gentle reminders, filling in the forgotten details with his own vivid imagination. They would laugh and make up new endings to their adventures, weaving a tapestry of whimsy that was uniquely their own.

Grandpa Henry's forgetfulness didn't stop them from embarking on new escapades.

They transformed everyday tasks into extraordinary quests, like searching for the lost socks in the mystical land of Dryerdom or battling the fierce dust bunnies that guarded the secret cookie jar.

Their playful spirits knew no bounds, and they reveled in the joy of each moment they shared. They would build forts out of couch cushions, have epic paper airplane races, and dance like no one was watching, creating cherished memories that would never fade.

Through their whimsical adventures, Grandpa Henry and Ethan discovered the true power of imagination. They realized that it wasn't the accuracy of the stories that mattered but the laughter, love, and togetherness they found along the way.

And as the sun would set on their fantastical journeys, Grandpa Henry would gather Ethan in his arms and whisper, «You, my dear grandson, are the hero of my heart. Our adventures may change, but the magic we create together will never fade.»

In the tale of Grandpa Henry and Ethan, they taught us that even when memories become fleeting, the bonds of love and imagination can light up the darkest corners. So, the next time you see a mischievous grandpa and his wide-eyed grandson, know that you are witnessing a timeless tale of connection, laughter, and the extraordinary power of a child's heart.

The Dress Surprise

Once upon a time, there lived a lively grandmother named Clara. Clara had a penchant for shopping and a delightful sense of adventure. One sunny afternoon, she decided to visit her favorite clothing store in search of a new dress.

As Clara perused the racks of colorful garments, a vibrant dress caught her eye. It was a beautiful floral print, and she instantly fell in love with its vibrant colors and flowing fabric. Without trying it on, Clara confidently purchased the dress, imagining how elegant she would look in it.

When Clara returned home, she couldn't contain her excitement. She carefully laid the dress on her bed, eager to show it off to her husband, Albert. Just as she arranged it with pride, Albert walked into the room, his eyes widening with surprise.

With a playful grin on his face, Albert chuckled and said, «Clara, did you buy us a tent? It looks like we're going camping!» Clara looked at him with confusion, her eyes darting between the dress and her husband's teasing expression.

Realization dawned on Clara, and they both burst into laughter. It turned out that Clara had mistakenly purchased a dress several sizes too large. The flowing fabric made it resemble a camping tent when laid out on the bed. They found humor in the situation and shared a moment of pure joy.

Clara couldn't help but laugh at her own enthusiasm, imagining herself as a glamorous camper. It became a funny anecdote that they would share with family and friends, always accompanied by laughter and lightheartedness.

Though the dress didn't fit as intended, Clara didn't let it dampen her spirits. She embraced the mishap and wore the dress proudly, letting its oversized charm add a touch of whimsy to her daily adventures.

In the story of «The Dress Surprise,» Clara reminds us that laughter is the best remedy for life's little surprises. Sometimes, even the most unexpected outcomes can become cherished memories. So, the next time you find yourself in a comical situation, channel Clara's spirit, embrace the laughter, and let joy be your guiding force.

And as for Clara and Albert, they continued to find merriment in the simplest of moments, creating a tapestry of laughter and love that adorned their lives like the vibrant threads of Clara's oversized dress.

The Dream Court: A Playful Journey to Justice

Once upon a time in the quiet town of Wellsboro, there lived a kind-hearted grandfather named Albert. From a young age, his heart swelled with a love for justice, and he had always dreamed of becoming a judge to promote fairness and order in his little corner of the world.

However, as the years went by, Albert found himself putting his dream on hold. He cared for his family and supported his grandchildren in their pursuits, but the idea of becoming a judge seemed more and more distant.

Albert's grandchildren, Emily and Jake, possessed vivid imaginations and a love for the theater. They were aware of their grandfather's dream and decided to do something special to help him experience the magic of a courtroom, even if only in a fictional way.

Combining their talents and love for their grandfather, Emily and Jake devised a small skit in which they played the roles of judges, lawyers, and witnesses. They gathered their family and loved ones to perform this special production, creating the illusion of a real courtroom.

The grandchildren meticulously planned every detail, from costumes to set design, and even scripted lines delivered with the fervor of young actors.

They poured all their energy and love into giving their grandfather a taste of fulfilling his long-held dream.

On the appointed evening, in the living room transformed into a courtroom, family and friends eagerly awaited the performance. Everyone was dressed as witnesses and jurors, and the mock trial began.

Emily, playing the role of a passionate attorney, fiercely defended her «client,» while Jake, exuding a regal presence, presided as the judge, delivering fair and just decisions. Other relatives and friends joined in as witnesses, each adding their own flair to the proceedings.

As the skit unfolded, Albert couldn't contain his joy and amazement. His grandchildren had brought his dream to life in the most creative and heartfelt way. He laughed, he applauded, and tears of gratitude welled up in his eyes.

In that intimate setting, surrounded by loved ones and immersed in the imaginative world of the courtroom, Albert felt the warmth of his grandchildren's love and support. Their playful endeavor became a symbol of the power of dreams, family bonds, and the importance of never letting go of one's aspirations.

From that day forward, whenever Albert reminisced about his dream, he would recall the magical evening when his grandchildren transformed his living room into a courthouse of hope and laughter. The memory would forever remind him that dreams could be realized, even in unexpected ways.

The Case of the Ticklish Feather

In a sleepy town nestled by a gentle river, lived a jovial old man named Mr. Henry. Mr. Henry had a contagious laugh that could brighten even the dullest of days. He was known for his playful nature and his love for tickling his friends with feathers. It was his way of spreading joy and laughter.

One sunny afternoon, Mr. Henry hatched a mischievous plan. He carefully concealed a feather in his pocket, waiting for the perfect moment to unleash his ticklish surprise. He decided to pay a visit to his dear friend, Mrs. Thompson, who was known for her hearty laughter.

As Mr. Henry entered Mrs. Thompson's cozy living room, he couldn't help but notice her peacefully reading a book. With a mischievous twinkle in his eye, he stealthily approached her armchair and gently tickled the back of her neck with the hidden feather.

Mrs. Thompson jolted in surprise, letting out a burst of laughter that echoed through the room. Confused but delighted, she looked around, trying to uncover the source of her sudden ticklish sensation. Mr. Henry stood nearby, grinning from ear to ear, unable to contain his laughter.

Realizing that Mr. Henry was the mastermind behind the ticklish encounter, Mrs. Thompson couldn't help but join in the merriment. From that day forward, their friendship blossomed with tickling escapades and contagious laughter.

The feather became a symbol of their playful bond and a reminder that laughter had the power to lighten any moment.

Whether it was a surprise tickle during a cup of tea or a feathered prank during a neighborhood gathering, Mr. Henry and Mrs. Thompson's mischievous laughter brightened the lives of those around them. Their playful antics brought joy and camaraderie to their tight-knit community, creating memories that would be cherished for years to come.

The Great Quest for Grandma's Glasses

Have you ever had one of those moments where you search high and low for something, only to realize it was right in front of you all along? Well, let me tell you the amusing tale of «The Great Quest for Grandma's Glasses.»

In a cozy little cottage, nestled amidst blooming gardens, lived a delightful grandmother named Edna. Every morning, she would sit in her favorite armchair, eager to read her beloved newspaper. However, there was one small problem – she couldn't find her glasses!

With a determined look on her face, Grandma Edna embarked on a quest to locate her spectacles. She searched the kitchen, rummaging through cabinets and drawers, hoping they had somehow found their way into the pantry. Alas, her glasses were nowhere to be found.

Undeterred, Grandma Edna moved to the living room, turning it upside down in her pursuit of the elusive eyewear. She combed through the cushions of the sofa, peeked under the coffee table, and even checked inside the vase of flowers, but her glasses were nowhere to be seen.

Growing a tad frustrated, Grandma Edna made her way to the bedroom, determined to unravel the mystery. She meticulously searched her dresser, looked beneath the pillows, and even checked inside her slippers, but her glasses remained elusive.

Just as Grandma Edna was about to give up hope, her mischievous cat, Whiskers, entered the room. Sensing her owner's distress, Whiskers pounced onto Grandma's lap, playfully pawing at her head. And that's when it happened – Grandma Edna felt something perched on her head. She reached up and, to her utter astonishment, discovered her missing glasses!

Giggling with delight, Grandma Edna realized that she had been wearing her glasses the entire time. How they ended up on top of her head, she could only guess. But the important thing was that her beloved glasses were finally found!

With a newfound clarity, Grandma Edna donned her spectacles and sat back in her armchair, finally able to read her cherished newspaper. As she leafed through the pages, she couldn't help but chuckle at the absurdity of her adventure.

From that day forward, Grandma Edna always made sure to check on top of her head before embarking on any search. And whenever she retold the tale of «The Great Quest for Grandma's Glasses,» laughter would fill the room, reminding everyone that sometimes the answers we seek are right under our noses.

The Remote Control Mischief

In a cozy living room, where memories were woven into the very fabric of the space, lived Grandpa Henry, a kind-hearted and forgetful soul. With a twinkle in his eye and a love for his favorite television shows, Grandpa Henry always sought comfort in the warmth of his armchair.

One evening, as the sun dipped below the horizon, Grandpa Henry settled into his armchair, eager to watch his beloved show. But as he reached for the remote control, he couldn't find it anywhere. Confusion etched across his face, and he began searching the room, leaving no cushion unturned.

«Have you seen my remote control, my dear?» Grandpa Henry called out to Grandma Martha, who was preparing a delicious meal in the kitchen.

Grandma Martha, with a hint of a smile, peeked her head into the living room and said, «Grandpa Henry, have you checked your hand? Sometimes, the best hiding spots are right in front of us.»

Grandpa Henry looked down at his hand and chuckled sheepishly. To his surprise, nestled snugly between his fingers was the elusive remote control. He burst into laughter, realizing the humor in his forgetful moment.

«Oh, silly me! The remote was right here in my hand all along. I must have been so eager to find it that I overlooked the obvious!» Grandpa Henry exclaimed, shaking his head in amusement.

Grandma Martha joined him in laughter, her eyes twinkling with affection. She knew that forgetfulness was a part of Grandpa Henry's charm, and she cherished every moment of their shared laughter.

From that day forward, Grandpa Henry and Grandma Martha continued to create countless lighthearted memories. The story of the hidden remote control became a delightful tale in their family, often shared with laughter and fondness.

It reminded them all of the importance of embracing life's little mishaps and finding joy in the simplest of moments. It taught them that sometimes, the keys to happiness could be right in our hands, waiting to be discovered.

The Great Caper

In the heart of Maplewood Manor, a charming retirement community filled with vibrant characters, lived a mischievous duo known as Charlie and Mildred. With their quick wit and playful spirits, they were always up to something that would leave the entire community laughing.

One sunny afternoon, as the residents gathered for their weekly game of bingo, Charlie and Mildred decided it was the perfect opportunity for a little caper. They glanced at each other, mischief dancing in their eyes, and whispered, «Have you ever played bingo with a twist?»

Curiosity piqued, the residents leaned in, eager to see what the mischievous duo had in store. Charlie, holding a deck of playing cards, announced, «Today, instead of bingo numbers, we will play with playing card suits!»

As the game began, laughter filled the room. The residents couldn't help but giggle as they shouted out suits like hearts, diamonds, clubs, and spades instead of traditional bingo numbers. Charlie and Mildred took turns impersonating the Queen of Hearts or the King of Clubs, adding a theatrical touch to the game.

The room buzzed with excitement and laughter as the residents embraced the unexpected twist. They cheered and clapped as their fellow players shouted, «I have a full house of diamonds!» or «Bingo! Four clubs in a row!»

Charlie and Mildred's ingenious caper turned a simple game of bingo into an uproarious affair. The residents reveled in the joy of camaraderie and the shared laughter that filled the room. They discovered that sometimes, it's the small and unexpected moments that bring the greatest delight.

As the game came to an end, Charlie and Mildred took a bow, grinning from ear to ear. The residents showered them with applause, grateful for the laughter and lightheartedness they had brought to their day.

From that day forward, Charlie and Mildred's bingo caper became a beloved tradition in Maplewood Manor. It served as a reminder that life is meant to be enjoyed, even in the simplest of activities. Laughter became the soundtrack of their community, connecting hearts and fostering a sense of belonging.

The story of «The Great Caper» spread beyond the walls of Maplewood Manor, bringing smiles to the faces of all who heard it. It inspired others to seek out the joy in unexpected places, to embrace their inner mischief-makers, and to create memories that would be cherished for a lifetime.

The Pillow Prank

Have you ever played a mischievous prank on someone you love? Well, let me tell you a hilarious story about Tommy, a playful grandson, and his unsuspecting grandmother, Grandma Lily.

One sunny afternoon, Tommy found himself bored and full of mischief. As he roamed through the house, his mischievous eyes landed on a fluffy pillow perched on the couch. An idea struck him like lightning – it was time for a prank!

Tommy tip-toed to the kitchen, trying to contain his laughter. He grabbed a nearby cushion and carefully tucked it under his shirt, creating a makeshift «belly.» With his secret weapon in place, he tiptoed back into the living room, where Grandma Lily was engrossed in her favorite book.

With a mischievous grin, Tommy approached Grandma Lily from behind. He raised the cushion «belly» high and let out a faux, exaggerated fart sound – PRRRRT! Startled, Grandma Lily jumped up, her eyes widening in surprise.

«Oh my!» she exclaimed, holding her hand over her mouth, a mix of shock and amusement on her face. Tommy burst into fits of laughter, unable to contain his joy at successfully pulling off the prank.

As Grandma Lily realized what had just happened, a smile crept onto her face, and she joined Tommy in his infectious laughter. They laughed and laughed, the sound of their shared joy filling the room.

From that day forward, Tommy and Grandma Lily developed a unique bond, filled with playful pranks and joyful laughter. They would often reminisce about the «pillow prank,» sharing countless moments of laughter and merriment.

The pillow prank became a treasured memory, a reminder of the special connection between a mischievous grandson and his spirited grandmother. It brought them closer together, fostering a sense of lightheartedness and playfulness that enriched their lives.

So, if you ever find yourself in the mood for a harmless prank, remember the story of Tommy and Grandma Lily. Embrace the joy of laughter, create unforgettable memories, and cherish the moments of laughter shared with your loved ones. After all, life is too short not to play a few pranks and fill the air with laughter and love.

The Tickling Troupe

Once upon a time, in a small village, there lived two mischievous friends named Emily and James. Their mischievous adventures were the talk of the town, and laughter seemed to follow them wherever they went.

One sunny afternoon, Emily devised a plan to surprise their beloved neighbor, Mrs. Jenkins. She knew Mrs. Jenkins had a contagious laughter that echoed through the neighborhood, and she wanted to witness it firsthand.

Emily and James gathered a group of friends, forming the mischievous «Tickling Troupe.» They hatched a plan to surprise Mrs. Jenkins with a tickle attack during her evening tea time.

As the clock struck six, the Tickling Troupe stealthily made their way to Mrs. Jenkins' house. They carefully positioned themselves around her cozy living room, waiting for the perfect moment to strike.

When Mrs. Jenkins sat down with her cup of tea, completely unaware of the impending tickle assault, the Tickling Troupe sprang into action. They tiptoed towards her, their fingers wiggling with anticipation.

Suddenly, the room erupted in giggles and laughter as Emily and her mischievous friends tickled Mrs. Jenkins from every angle. Mrs. Jenkins, caught off guard, couldn't control her laughter, and it filled the room like music.

She squirmed and laughed, trying to fend off the tickles, but the Tickling Troupe was relentless. They tickled her under the arms, behind the knees, and even on the soles of her feet, causing her laughter to reach new heights.

The joyful chaos continued for what felt like an eternity, until finally, Mrs. Jenkins pleaded for mercy amidst fits of laughter. The Tickling Troupe, satisfied with their successful mission, ceased their tickling frenzy and collapsed on the floor, joining Mrs. Jenkins in uncontrollable laughter.

As their laughter subsided, Mrs. Jenkins wiped away tears of joy and said, «Oh, you mischievous bunch! You certainly know how to brighten an old lady's day. My cheeks ache from all the laughter!»

Emily, beaming with pride, replied, «We knew your laughter was contagious, Mrs. Jenkins, and we couldn't resist joining in the fun.»

From that day on, the Tickling Troupe became legends in the village, known for their hilarious pranks and their ability to bring laughter to the hearts of all. Their tickle attack on Mrs. Jenkins became a cherished memory, shared with laughter at every gathering.

The story of the Tickling Troupe reminded everyone of the power of laughter and the joy that comes from shared mischief. It taught them that sometimes, a tickle can be the best medicine for the soul.

The Topsy-Turvy Recipe: A Hilarious Culinary Adventure

Once upon a time, in a cozy little kitchen, lived Grandma Mildred, a passionate cook with a flair for adventure. She loved trying new recipes and surprising her family with delicious meals. One day, she stumbled upon a unique recipe for a mouthwatering dessert called «Triple Chocolate Surprise.» Excited to give it a try, she gathered all the ingredients.

As Grandma Mildred carefully measured and mixed the dry ingredients, her mischievous cat, Whiskers, leaped onto the kitchen counter. Whiskers couldn't resist the sight of the fluffy cocoa powder, and before Grandma knew it, he batted it off the counter, sending it flying through the air. Grandma chuckled and exclaimed, «Oh, Whiskers, you've added your own touch of magic to the recipe!»

Undeterred, Grandma continued her baking adventure. She added the wet ingredients and whisked them together with a determined grin. But just as she was about to pour the mixture into the baking dish, she realized she had forgotten the main ingredient—chocolate! She searched high and low, checking every cupboard and drawer, but no chocolate was to be found.

Grandma sighed and laughed at her forgetfulness. «Well, well, it seems the 'Triple Chocolate Surprise' will have to be a 'Double Surprise' today! We'll just have to make do without the third chocolate.»

With a shrug and a smile, Grandma poured the batter into the baking dish and popped it into the oven. The aroma of chocolate filled the kitchen, and anticipation grew among the family members. When the timer finally beeped, Grandma pulled out the slightly imperfect, yet delicious-looking dessert.

As the family gathered around the table and took their first bites, they couldn't help but be amazed. The «Double Surprise» dessert was absolutely scrumptious! It had just the right balance of sweetness and richness, even without the third chocolate.

They laughed and savored each bite, savoring the unexpected twist in the recipe. Grandma Mildred had unintentionally created a new family favorite—a dessert that showcased her ingenuity and ability to turn mishaps into delicious triumphs.

From that day forward, the «Double Surprise» became a regular treat at Grandma Mildred's table. It served as a reminder that sometimes, the most memorable and enjoyable experiences come from unexpected surprises and the ability to adapt and make the best out of any situation.

And so, with a heart full of laughter and a kitchen full of love, Grandma Mildred continued to whip up culinary adventures, always ready to embrace the joy that comes from a little bit of chaos and a whole lot of deliciousness.

The Elusive Walking Cane

In a cozy little house, nestled among the rolling hills, lived an endearing grandfather named Henry. Henry had a favorite walking cane that had been with him through thick and thin. It was more than just a cane to him; it was a trusted companion on his daily walks.

One sunny morning, as Henry prepared for his walk, he couldn't find his beloved cane anywhere. He searched high and low, rummaging through drawers and peering behind furniture, but it was nowhere to be found. Frustrated yet determined, he enlisted the help of his mischievous grandchildren, Emma and Jack.

Emma and Jack, with their eyes sparkling with excitement, joined the search party. They combed through every nook and cranny of the house, turning it upside down in their quest to locate the missing cane. But to their surprise, it was nowhere to be seen.

Just as they were about to give up, Emma's gaze fell upon the most unexpected sight. There, in the corner of the living room, stood Henry's walking cane—bright, conspicuous, and impossible to miss. The children burst into fits of laughter, unable to contain their amusement at the comical turn of events.

Henry, puzzled, followed their gaze and discovered the source of their laughter. There, in plain sight, was his walking cane, leaning against the wall as if it had been waiting to be found all along.

His face flushed with embarrassment, but he couldn't help but join in the laughter, realizing the irony of the situation.

The trio burst into uncontrollable laughter, their joy echoing through the house. Henry couldn't believe how he had overlooked his cherished cane, which had been right under his nose the entire time. It became a running joke in the family, a tale that would be retold with laughter during family gatherings for years to come.

From that day forward, whenever Henry went on his walks, he made sure to keep a watchful eye on his walking cane, placing it prominently by the door as a reminder of the day he had searched high and low for something that was hiding in plain sight.

The laughter and light-heartedness that accompanied the search for the elusive walking cane served as a reminder to Henry and his grandchildren that sometimes, the things we search for the most fervently are right in front of us, waiting to be noticed.

And so, as Henry continued his walks with his beloved walking cane by his side, he carried not only the support it provided but also the memory of that unforgettable day. It became a symbol of laughter, family bonds, and the delightful moments that can emerge from the simplest of mishaps.

The Hidden Treasures: Grandma's Mischief

In a quaint little house, nestled amidst a garden of blooming flowers, lived a spirited and mischievous kitten named Pumpkin. With bright green eyes and a fluffy orange coat, Pumpkin had a knack for turning everyday moments into grand adventures.

One sunny afternoon, Grandma Rose decided to wear her cherished pearl necklace, a treasured family heirloom. She opened her jewelry box, only to find it empty. Her heart skipped a beat as she realized her beloved pearls were missing.

Frantically searching the house, Grandma Rose couldn't help but notice the mischievous glint in Pumpkin's eyes. A playful thought crossed her mind. Could it be possible that Pumpkin was behind the disappearance of her precious pearls?

With a twinkle in her eye, Grandma Rose decided to play along. She turned to Pumpkin and asked, «Oh, Pumpkin, have you seen my pearls? They seem to have disappeared. I hope you haven't been up to any mischief!»

Pumpkin tilted her head and let out a soft meow, almost as if she understood Grandma Rose's words. She darted off into the house, her tiny paws silently padding on the floor.

Grandma Rose followed Pumpkin, a smile tugging at the corners of her lips. She watched as Pumpkin expertly maneuvered through the house, leading her on a playful chase.

As they explored every nook and cranny, Grandma Rose couldn't help but admire Pumpkin's agility and curiosity. It was as if Pumpkin had transformed into a mischievous detective on a quest to unravel the mystery.

Finally, they arrived in the cozy corner of the living room, where Pumpkin paused by a decorative flower vase. To Grandma Rose's surprise, nestled among the flowers were her missing pearls, glistening in the sunlight.

Grandma Rose burst into laughter, realizing that Pumpkin had hidden her pearls as part of their playful game. «Oh, you sly little trickster! You wanted to make finding my pearls an adventure, didn't you?»

Pumpkin purred contentedly, her tail swaying back and forth as if proud of her clever hiding spot.

From that day on, Grandma Rose and Pumpkin shared a special bond. They continued their playful escapades, with Pumpkin occasionally hiding small trinkets and Grandma Rose joining in the search, always ending in laughter and the joy of discovery.

The story of Grandma Rose and Pumpkin's hidden treasures became a beloved tale in their family. It reminded them all of the importance of embracing playfulness and finding delight in the simplest moments. It taught them that sometimes, a mischievous kitten could lead you to the most precious treasures of all—joy, laughter, and the enduring bond between a grandmother and her playful companion.

The Joyful Recipe Adventurer

In a cozy kitchen that overflowed with warmth and tantalizing aromas, lived a remarkable grandmother named Evelyn. Her love for cooking was unmatched, but her memory often played tricks on her. However, this didn't deter her spirit or her infectious smile that brightened every corner of her world.

Each day, Evelyn would embark on culinary adventures, armed with recipe cards and a determined spirit. As she sifted through the pages, her eyes would dance with excitement and anticipation. But sometimes, the ingredients would slip through the sieve of her memory.

Undeterred, Evelyn would giggle at her forgetfulness and embrace the opportunity to embark on a creative journey. She would gather her loved ones around, turning the kitchen into a stage for laughter and culinary improvisation.

One day, as she attempted to recreate her famous apple pie, Evelyn found herself staring at an empty bowl. The apples she had planned to use had vanished from her mind. With a playful grin, she exclaimed, «Who needs apples when we have the sweetest memories to fill our pies!»

Her family joined in the laughter, transforming the traditional apple pie into a canvas for collective creativity. They tossed in a handful of cherries, a sprinkle of cinnamon, and a dash of love. The resulting pie became a symbol of resilience and the power of adaptability.

Evelyn's contagious joy and unwavering spirit inspired those around her. Friends and family eagerly volunteered to be her kitchen assistants, helping her gather ingredients and ensuring the recipe stayed on track. With every culinary mishap, they turned it into an opportunity to invent new flavors and create memories that would last a lifetime.

Despite her forgetfulness, Evelyn's kitchen became a place of connection, where cherished family recipes mingled with laughter and unbounded love. Her joyful demeanor taught her loved ones that life's imperfections could be transformed into delightful surprises and delicious moments of togetherness.

As the years passed, Evelyn's kitchen became a hub of love and laughter, attracting friends and neighbors who yearned for the joy she radiated. Her renowned «Memory-Making Meals» became legendary, not for their adherence to traditional recipes, but for the stories they told and the smiles they evoked.

Evelyn, the joyful recipe adventurer, showed the world that a forgetful memory could never overshadow the happiness that lies within. Her culinary escapades taught everyone the beauty of embracing the unexpected, cherishing every moment, and savoring life's flavorful journey.

The Whistling Teapot

Have you ever encountered an object that seemed to have a mind of its own? Let me share with you the delightful tale of Mrs. Thompson and her mischievous teapot.

Mrs. Thompson was an avid tea drinker who cherished her daily ritual of brewing a warm cup of tea. One day, she brought home a new teapot with a unique quirk – it had a tendency to whistle at the most unexpected moments.

As Mrs. Thompson filled the teapot with water and placed it on the stove, she couldn't help but wonder what surprises awaited her. Sure enough, as the water reached its boiling point, the teapot let out a loud, melodic whistle that echoed throughout the kitchen.

Amused by the unexpected symphony, Mrs. Thompson couldn't resist giggling at the teapot's lively personality. From that day forward, every time she made tea, she eagerly awaited the whimsical whistle.

Word spread quickly about Mrs. Thompson's whistling teapot, and soon friends and neighbors would gather in her kitchen just to witness the delightful spectacle. They would exchange stories and laughter, all while savoring the comforting aroma of freshly brewed tea.

The teapot seemed to have a mischievous charm, turning ordinary tea time into a lively and memorable experience.

It brought people together, fostering a sense of joy and camaraderie that warmed their hearts.

As the years went by, Mrs. Thompson's teapot became a cherished symbol of friendship and shared laughter. It became a tradition for guests to bring their favorite tea leaves, eager to hear the whimsical whistle and create lasting memories.

The whistling teapot taught Mrs. Thompson an important lesson – sometimes, it's the unexpected quirks and surprises in life that bring us the most joy. It reminded her to embrace the spontaneity and find humor in the everyday moments, transforming them into cherished memories.

So, the next time you enjoy a cup of tea, remember the tale of Mrs. Thompson and her mischievous teapot. Embrace the unexpected melodies that life brings, gather your loved ones, and let laughter fill the air as you create your own magical moments.

The Football Rivalry of Grandpa Joe and Grandpa Frank

Grandpa Joe and Grandpa Frank, united by their love for football, formed an unbreakable bond. Despite being passionate supporters of rival teams, their friendly rivalry brought laughter and excitement to their lives.

Week after week, the two friends gathered at Joe's house, dressed in their team's colors, to watch the much-anticipated football matches. Their room echoed with cheers, shouts, and good-natured banter, creating a lively atmosphere.

As time passed, Joe's memory began to fade, and Frank's eyesight declined. However, their shared passion for football remained unwavering. Determined to continue enjoying the game together, they found creative ways to adapt.

One sunny day, Joe had a brilliant idea. He transformed his backyard into a makeshift football field, complete with mini-goal posts and foam balls. Joe invited Frank over for a special match, and they eagerly embraced the challenge.

With childlike enthusiasm, Joe and Frank ran, kicked, and scored goals on their improvised field. They laughed at their mistakes and celebrated each other's triumphs. Their love for the sport transcended any limitations brought by age.

During breaks, they would sit on the porch, reminiscing about legendary football players and engaging in friendly debates.

Their conversations were filled with shared memories and witty exchanges, bringing endless joy to their friendship.

One day, as they sat together, Joe struggled to remember the name of a player they used to idolize. Instead of becoming frustrated, they turned it into a game, creating hilarious nicknames for the forgotten player. Their laughter filled the air, showcasing their quick wit.

Their football gatherings became a testament to the enduring power of friendship and the joy found in shared passions. Joe and Frank may have forgotten some details, but their bond remained unbreakable.

Their love for football and their unwavering support for rival teams inspired their families and friends. Their spirit brought generations together, teaching the true meaning of sportsmanship and the joy of camaraderie.

In the end, their matches weren't solely about winning or losing; they were about the friendship that surpassed football rivalries. Joe and Frank taught everyone the value of sportsmanship, cheering for their teams while cherishing each other's company.

As the years passed, their football matches continued, their love for the game undiminished. Even as memories faded and eyesight grew weaker, Joe and Frank remained a team, exemplifying the enduring power of friendship.

Grandpa's Golfing Adventure

In the quaint town of Fairview, there lived a sprightly and adventurous grandfather named Henry. Despite his age, Henry's love for outdoor activities burned bright, and his favorite pastime was playing golf. He would often regale his grandchildren with tales of his golfing triumphs and daring shots.

One sunny Saturday morning, Henry decided to invite his grandson, Max, for a memorable day of golfing. Max, eager to spend time with his beloved grandpa, jumped at the opportunity.

They arrived at the local golf course, greeted by lush green fairways and a gentle breeze that whispered promises of a fun-filled day. Henry, donning his signature plaid golfing pants and a mischievous grin, led Max to the first tee.

As Henry prepared to swing his club, he couldn't resist adding a touch of flair to his shot. With a twinkle in his eye, he took a few exaggerated practice swings, imitating the golfing legends he had admired for years. Max watched in awe, his eyes widening with anticipation.

With a mighty swing, Henry sent the golf ball soaring through the air. However, instead of gracefully landing on the fairway, it veered off-course, bouncing off a tree branch and landing in a nearby pond with an amusing splash.

Henry and Max burst into laughter, unable to contain their amusement at the unexpected turn of events.

The nearby golfers turned their heads, curious about the source of the uproarious laughter. Unfazed by the mishap, Henry embraced the moment, exclaiming, «That's what I call a hole-in-one, aquatic edition!»

Undeterred by the comical incident, Henry and Max continued their golfing expedition. As they moved from hole to hole, Henry's enthusiasm was infectious. He shared tales of golfing legends and imparted wisdom about the game, all while relishing in the joy of spending quality time with his grandson.

Throughout the day, Henry's shots provided moments of laughter and surprise. From landing in sand traps to ricocheting off unsuspecting birdhouses, each swing held the promise of a hilarious outcome. Yet, despite the occasional misfires, Henry's spirit remained unyielding, and his love for the game shone through.

As the sun began to set, Henry and Max completed their final hole. They walked off the course, their hearts full of cherished memories and their faces beaming with smiles. Henry patted Max on the back and said, «No matter where the ball lands, the real victory is the joy we find along the way.»

Years passed, and Max grew to love golf just as much as his grandfather did. He would often recount the tales of their golfing adventure, bringing laughter and warmth to family gatherings. The legacy of Henry's playful approach to the game lived on, inspiring future generations to embrace the spirit of fun and laughter in all their endeavors.

The Unforgettable Surprise

In a cozy little house nestled in a quiet neighborhood, lived a charming old man named Henry. Henry was known for his warm heart, gentle demeanor, and his occasional bouts of forgetfulness. Despite his age, he maintained a childlike curiosity about the world around him and a love for simple joys.

One sunny morning, as the birds chirped outside his window, Henry woke up feeling content but couldn't shake the feeling that something important was looming in the air. He went about his usual routine, brewing a fresh cup of coffee and tending to his beloved garden, hoping the elusive thought would find its way back to him.

Meanwhile, Henry's family, led by his mischievous grandchildren, Sarah and Jack, were busy planning a surprise for his upcoming birthday. They scurried around, decorating the house with balloons, wrapping gifts, and preparing a delicious feast fit for a king. They wanted to make this birthday one that Henry would never forget.

As the day progressed, Henry found himself engaged in various activities, from tinkering in his workshop to sharing stories with his cherished neighbors. However, the nagging feeling persisted, and he couldn't quite put his finger on what he was forgetting.

Little did he know, his family had been carefully orchestrating the surprise celebration in the backyard.

The decorations sparkled in the sunlight, and the air was filled with anticipation and excitement. Sarah and Jack eagerly awaited their grandpa's arrival, eager to witness his reaction to the surprise.

As the evening descended, Henry returned home, a slight smile playing on his lips. The front door creaked open, revealing the joyous faces of his family, all gathered together to celebrate his special day. Confusion swept over Henry's face, and for a moment, he couldn't comprehend the scene before him.

«Surprise!» they shouted in unison, as laughter and cheers filled the room. Henry's eyes widened with astonishment and delight. He had completely forgotten about his birthday, but his family had not. They had transformed his ordinary day into an extraordinary celebration of love, laughter, and cherished memories.

Henry's heart swelled with gratitude as he embraced each family member, feeling the warmth of their love and the happiness radiating through the room. His grandchildren, Sarah and Jack, couldn't contain their excitement, proudly presenting him with handmade cards and thoughtful gifts.

As the night unfolded, Henry's family regaled him with tales of their preparations, sharing laughter and creating new memories. It was a reminder that sometimes the most precious moments are born from the unexpected, and that even in forgetfulness, love and family can fill the gaps and create unforgettable experiences. From that day forward, Henry cherished every moment, holding onto the love and joy that surrounded him.

Clara's Courageous Flight

Clara, the adventurous chicken, had always dreamed of soaring through the sky like the birds she admired. She often gazed longingly at the flock of seagulls that gracefully glided above the ocean waves. Clara yearned for the freedom and exhilaration that flying promised.

One sunny day, as Clara pecked at grains in the barnyard, she noticed a peculiar contraption tucked away in a forgotten corner. It was an old kite, worn but sturdy. Inspiration sparked within Clara's feathery heart.

With determination in her eyes, Clara set out to make her dream come true. She studied the kite, examining its structure and understanding how it harnessed the wind. Clara, being a resourceful chicken, found some string and carefully attached it to the kite.

The breeze picked up, and Clara knew it was her chance. She flapped her wings vigorously, running against the wind. With a leap, she took flight, gripping the string tightly in her claws. The kite lifted her off the ground, carrying her into the sky.

Clara soared higher and higher, her heart filled with pure joy. She marveled at the world below, the patchwork fields, and the bustling farm. The other animals watched in awe as Clara sailed through the air, a vision of bravery and determination.

As Clara gracefully glided above, the seagulls noticed her.

They were impressed by her audacity and invited her to join their aerial dance. Clara, without hesitation, accepted their invitation, and together they performed a dazzling display of synchronized flight.

Clara's courage and willingness to pursue her dream inspired the animals on the farm. They realized that no dream was too big or too far-fetched. They, too, began to pursue their aspirations, finding the strength within themselves to overcome their fears.

After a breathtaking flight, Clara gently descended, landing back in the barnyard. The animals cheered and applauded her triumphant return. Clara, with a beaming smile, thanked her newfound seagull friends and cherished the memory of her incredible adventure.

From that day forward, Clara became a symbol of bravery and determination on the farm. She taught everyone the importance of pursuing their dreams, no matter how impossible they may seem.

The Melodies of Remembrance

In a quiet corner of the nursing home, amidst the soft hum of laughter and gentle conversations, lived Martha, a spirited woman with a heart full of melodies. Though her memory flickered like a candle in the wind, her love for music remained a steadfast beacon of joy in her life.

Martha's days were filled with the timeless tunes of yesteryears. With every step she took, a forgotten melody danced on her lips. But as her memory faded, the lyrics often eluded her grasp, leaving her hums incomplete.

One day, a young caregiver named Sarah noticed Martha's love for music and hatched a heartwarming plan. Sarah gathered a group of volunteers, musicians from the local community, who shared a passion for spreading the healing power of music. Together, they formed a makeshift band called «The Harmonious Memories.»

Every week, the band would visit Martha and other residents with dementia, filling the air with enchanting melodies. As the first notes resonated through the room, Martha's eyes sparkled with recognition, her soul awakening to the timeless tunes.

In the company of «The Harmonious Memories,» Martha's memory transcended its limitations. She would join the band, tambourine in hand, and sway to the rhythm. The lyrics, once lost in the depths of her mind, found their way back to her lips as she sang with newfound exuberance.

The magic of music weaved a tapestry of emotions within the hearts of the residents. Laughter and tears mingled as forgotten memories resurfaced, carried by the harmonies and lyrics that had become the threads of their lives.

As the band played on, Martha's spirit soared. With each passing session, her confidence grew, and she began to compose her own melodies, capturing fragments of her journey through life. The room transformed into a haven of creativity and joy, where the music became a bridge between past and present, weaving a tapestry of shared experiences.

The impact of «The Harmonious Memories» extended beyond the nursing home walls. Families marveled at the transformation in their loved ones, witnessing the power of music to stir memories and awaken dormant emotions. The community rallied around the band, embracing the belief that even in the face of forgetfulness, the soul's connection to music remained unbreakable.

Martha's melodies became the anthem of hope, reminding everyone that while memories might fade, the essence of who we are can be expressed through the universal language of music. Her journey taught them that in the absence of words, the power of melodies could bridge the gap, reaching deep into the recesses of the heart.

And so, «The Harmonious Memories» continued their mission, sharing the gift of music with those touched by dementia. Through their enchanting melodies, they brought solace, inspiration, and a reminder that the essence of our being can never truly be lost, as long as the songs within our hearts continue to echo.

The Adventures of Mr. Thompson

Once upon a time in a cozy retirement home, resided Mr. Thompson, a mischievous and curious soul with a mischievous twinkle in his eyes. Despite the fog of dementia that often clouded his thoughts, he embraced each day as a new adventure.

Mr. Thompson's antics brought laughter and joy to the residents and staff alike. One sunny afternoon, he embarked on a quest to find the hidden treasure rumored to be buried within the nursing home's garden. Armed with a homemade treasure map scribbled on a scrap of paper, he set off with unwavering determination.

As he shuffled through the corridors, he bumped into Mrs. Jenkins, a fellow resident known for her sharp wit and quick humor. She joined Mr. Thompson on his quest, her laughter infectious as they delved into their grand adventure.

Together, they followed the clues on the map, stumbling upon unexpected surprises along the way. The garden transformed into a jungle, teeming with imaginary creatures and hidden treasures. They encountered mischievous squirrels, who joined their merry chase, and even unearthed a hidden stash of acorns.

Their laughter echoed through the halls, drawing others to join the whimsical escapade. The residents and staff, young and old, embraced the childlike wonder that had awoken in their hearts. They raced across the garden, chasing rainbows and sharing stories of forgotten dreams.

As the sun began to set, Mr. Thompson and Mrs. Jenkins returned to reality, their treasure hunt coming to an end. But the memories they created lingered, etched in the collective spirit of the retirement home. The garden had become a portal to a world where age and ailments held no power, where the joy of the present moment surpassed any limitations of the mind.

From that day forward, Mr. Thompson and Mrs. Jenkins continued their adventures, exploring new realms of imagination and laughter. Their playful spirits became beacons of inspiration, reminding everyone that even amidst the challenges of aging and dementia, the soul's capacity for joy and adventure remained unyielding.

The tale of Mr. Thompson's garden treasure became legendary within the walls of the retirement home. It became a symbol of the power of imagination, friendship, and embracing the present moment with childlike enthusiasm. Each day brought new adventures, as residents embarked on journeys filled with laughter, wonder, and the belief that life's most precious treasures could be found in the simplest of moments.

And so, the spirit of Mr. Thompson lived on, a reminder that age was just a number, and the truest adventures were the ones that unfolded within our hearts and minds. The residents of the retirement home learned to cherish the magic of the present, cherishing each day as a grand adventure waiting to be discovered.

The Mismatched Sock Tradition

One sunny afternoon, Grandpa Harold set out on a visit to his beloved grandchildren. With excitement in his heart and a skip in his step, he couldn't wait to spend the day with them. But there was one tiny problem that left him scratching his head – he couldn't find a matching pair of socks!

Grandpa Harold rummaged through his drawer, searching high and low, but every sock he found seemed to have lost its partner. Chuckling to himself, he shrugged and decided to wear mismatched socks instead. After all, life was too short to worry about perfectly coordinated footwear.

When Grandpa Harold arrived at his grandchildren's house, they greeted him with open arms and bright smiles. As he took off his shoes, they noticed his mismatched socks and burst into laughter. Instead of feeling embarrassed, Grandpa Harold joined in the laughter, joking that his socks had taken on a rebellious spirit.

Curiosity sparked in the eyes of the grandchildren, and they couldn't resist the temptation to join Grandpa Harold's mismatched sock revolution. They ran to their rooms, eagerly returning with their own assortment of mismatched socks, showcasing patterns, colors, and sizes that defied all conventions.

From that day forward, mismatched socks became a cherished tradition whenever Grandpa Harold visited.

Each time he came over, the grandchildren would eagerly raid their sock drawers, deliberately selecting socks that didn't match. They reveled in the joy of embracing individuality and celebrating the uniqueness of their family bond.

As the years passed, the tradition grew stronger. Grandpa Harold's grandchildren became young adults, yet they never outgrew the whimsical charm of mismatched socks. They continued the tradition even when they had families of their own, passing down the laughter and camaraderie to the next generation.

The mismatched socks became a symbol of their love, unity, and the importance of embracing life's little quirks. It was a reminder that perfection wasn't necessary to create beautiful memories and that the most cherished moments often arose from unexpected circumstances.

Grandpa Harold's visits were always filled with laughter, warmth, and the joy of being together. The sight of mismatched socks became a familiar and cherished sight, a testament to their family's ability to find happiness in the simplest of things.

And so, the tradition of wearing mismatched socks lived on, generation after generation. It reminded them that life was too short to worry about the small things, and that true happiness could be found in the loving company of family and the laughter that echoed through their hearts.

The Mischievous Umbrella

Have you ever had a mischievous encounter with an inanimate object? Well, let me tell you the amusing tale of Mr. Johnson and his unforgettable adventure with an umbrella.

One rainy afternoon, Mr. Johnson found himself caught in a sudden downpour while strolling through the city. Determined to stay dry, he quickly ducked into a nearby store and purchased a bright red umbrella. Little did he know that this seemingly ordinary umbrella had a mischievous personality of its own.

As Mr. Johnson continued his walk, he noticed that his new umbrella had a habit of turning inside out at the slightest gust of wind. Each time a strong breeze blew, the umbrella would flip upside down, leaving Mr. Johnson struggling to regain control.

Passersby couldn't help but chuckle as they watched Mr. Johnson's comical struggle against the rebellious umbrella. Undeterred by the persistent mishaps, Mr. Johnson refused to give up on his new rain companion.

The umbrella seemed to have a mischievous charm that brought laughter to those around him. People on the street began to anticipate Mr. Johnson's encounters with the unpredictable umbrella, eagerly awaiting the entertaining spectacle.

Mr. Johnson, with his sense of humor intact, embraced the unexpected amusement. He even started adding his own twist to the performance, incorporating funny dance moves and exaggerated gestures as he battled the rebellious umbrella.

Soon, Mr. Johnson became a local sensation, known as «The Dancing Umbrella Man.» People would line the streets, eagerly awaiting his impromptu performances. With a twinkle in his eye and a smile on his face, he turned an ordinary rainy day into a delightful spectacle of laughter and joy.

The mischievous umbrella taught Mr. Johnson an important lesson – life is full of unexpected twists and turns, and sometimes it's best to embrace the chaos and find humor in the midst of it all. It reminded him that even in the face of challenges and mishaps, a positive attitude and a willingness to laugh can turn any situation into a memorable adventure.

So, the next time you find yourself caught in the rain with an unruly umbrella, remember Mr. Johnson and his mischievous companion. Embrace the unexpected, find joy in the laughter it brings, and let your inner light shine through, just like «The Dancing Umbrella Man.»

Grandma and Granddaughter's Delightful Adventures

In a quaint little town, resided Grandma Beatrice and her curious granddaughter, Lily, an inseparable duo on whimsical adventures that brought laughter and joy to their lives. One sunny afternoon, they decided to have a picnic in their enchanting backyard garden. With a basket filled with delicious sandwiches, juicy fruits, and homemade lemonade, they set off on a delightful escapade.

As they settled under the shade of a big oak tree, Grandma shared tales of her childhood adventures. Lily listened with wide-eyed wonder, imagining herself in those magical moments. They giggled, shared secrets, and created cherished memories.

Their picnic turned into a mischievous adventure when a squirrel named Nutty stole their sandwich. Grandma and Lily chased the speedy thief, playfully naming him the «Sandwich Bandit» and vowing to guard their food in future picnics.

Their next escapade took them to a farm, where they met an adorable baby lamb. Lily hugged the fluffy creature, and they spent the day exploring the farm, petting animals, and attempting to milk a cow, resulting in hilarious outcomes.

As seasons changed, their adventures transformed. They danced in the rain, built sandcastles at the beach, and had a magical camping trip under the starlit sky, sharing laughter and ghost stories.

Throughout their escapades, Grandma Beatrice taught Lily the importance of kindness, imagination, and finding beauty in the world. Lily reminded her grandma to embrace childlike wonder.

Their bond grew stronger, and they realized that the greatest adventure was simply being together. Baking cookies, exploring nature, and having silly dance parties filled their days with cherished memories.

So, if you encounter Grandma Beatrice and Lily, be prepared to join their delightful adventures. They'll show you the magic in everyday moments, the joy of simple pleasures, and the power of an unbreakable bond between generations. In their world, the ordinary becomes extraordinary, and each day holds laughter, love, and endless possibilities.

The Suit Mismatch: A Hilarious Fashion Adventure

«Have you ever tried on clothes that seemed to be tailored for someone else entirely? Let me tell you a story about Harold, who found himself in such a situation.

One day, Harold set out to buy a new suit for his long-awaited party. He wanted to impress his friends and feel stylish and confident. However, being a person with a great sense of humor, Harold always found himself on the edge of a comical adventure.

When Harold arrived at the store and began trying on different suits, he noticed something peculiar. None of them fit him properly. Harold stood in front of the mirror, laughing uncontrollably, while the suit sleeves were too short, the pants were too long, and the jacket seemed like it belonged to a giant.

People passing by couldn't help but join in his laughter. The store assistants, initially puzzled, eventually joined the merriment, realizing the hilarious mismatch. Harold turned his shopping trip into an impromptu fashion show, showcasing a series of comically ill-fitting suits.

As the laughter subsided, Harold thanked the store staff for their patience and humor. He left the store, not with a suit that fit perfectly, but with memories of a day filled with laughter and joy.

From that day forward, whenever Harold attended a party, he became known as the man who could make anyone laugh, whether it was through his witty jokes or his knack for finding mismatched clothes. And he embraced his unique style with pride, reminding everyone that sometimes the best moments in life come from embracing the unexpected and finding humor in the quirkiest situations.

So, the next time you try on an outfit that doesn't quite fit, remember Harold's story and let yourself laugh along with the unexpected twists that life brings.» I hope you enjoy this story! Let me know if there's anything else I can assist you with.

The Unforgettable Picnic: A Tale of Mismatched Tastes

Once upon a time, in a serene countryside, resided two best friends, Martha and Henry. Despite their old age and battle with dementia, they cherished their bond and shared countless unforgettable moments. One sunny day, they decided to embark on a delightful picnic adventure.

Martha and Henry carefully packed their wicker basket with tasty treats, making sure to include all their favorites. But there was one little twist—they had forgotten to coordinate their choices! As they set off to find the perfect spot under a shady tree, they realized their picnic basket was filled with an odd assortment of mismatched foods.

Henry eagerly pulled out a jar of tangy pickles, a tin of sardines, and a loaf of crusty bread. Martha, on the other hand, discovered a box of colorful macarons, a jar of strawberry jam, and a jug of sparkling lemonade. They both looked at each other, puzzled yet amused by the contrasting spread.

Unfazed by the culinary disarray, Martha and Henry embraced the moment with laughter. They decided to make the best of their peculiar feast, combining unexpected flavors and creating a unique dining experience. With each bite, they shared their honest opinions, savoring the peculiar taste combinations.

As they nibbled on pickles with macarons, and took sips of lemonade followed by sardines, the giggles grew louder.

Passersby couldn't help but smile at the sight of two dear friends relishing their eccentric picnic. Martha and Henry's joy radiated, turning their unusual menu into a delightful spectacle.

Soon, other park visitors gathered around, curious to taste the unconventional pairing. Martha and Henry became the center of attention, sharing laughter, stories, and their mismatched culinary adventures with newfound friends. The picnic transformed into a vibrant celebration of spontaneity, where taste boundaries blurred and laughter flourished.

From that day forward, Martha and Henry's mismatched picnic became a cherished tradition in the park. People from all walks of life would join in, bringing their own unusual food combinations, eager to experience the magic of unexpected flavors and shared laughter.

As time passed, Martha and Henry's memories faded, but the spirit of their mismatched picnic lived on. The park became a place where people set aside their culinary preferences and embraced the joy of trying something new. It was a testament to the power of laughter, friendship, and the ability to find delight in the most unexpected places.

And so, in that peaceful corner of the countryside, the aroma of pickles and macarons mingled, and laughter echoed through the trees, reminding everyone that life's most memorable moments often emerge from the most delightful mismatches.

The Mysterious Adventures of Granny Edna

Granny Edna was no ordinary grandmother. With a mischievous sparkle in her eyes and a heart full of curiosity, she embarked on daily adventures that kept her young at heart. Despite her advancing age and occasional bouts of forgetfulness, Granny Edna embraced life with a zest for exploration.

One fine summer morning, Granny Edna woke up with an intriguing idea. She decided to become a treasure hunter in her own home. Armed with a treasure map she had drawn herself, Granny Edna embarked on a quest to find hidden treasures.

As she tiptoed through her house, Granny Edna followed the clues she had scattered throughout the rooms. The first clue led her to the living room, where she discovered a secret compartment in an old bookshelf. Inside, she found a collection of forgotten trinkets and childhood mementos.

With each clue she deciphered, Granny Edna unearthed more treasures, both tangible and intangible. She discovered a box of love letters from her late husband, reminding her of the deep bond they shared. A dusty photo album revealed cherished memories of family vacations and joyful celebrations.

But the true treasure for Granny Edna wasn't in the physical artifacts she uncovered. It was the flood of emotions and memories that resurfaced with each find. She laughed and cried, reliving the moments that shaped her life.

As she ventured into the attic, Granny Edna stumbled upon an old chest filled with costumes and props from her days as a theater enthusiast. Without a second thought, she dressed up as a whimsical pirate, complete with an eye patch and a parrot on her shoulder.

With her newfound pirate persona, Granny Edna set sail on a make-believe voyage in her own backyard. She imagined sailing the high seas, searching for buried treasure and encountering fantastical creatures along the way. Passersby couldn't help but smile as they witnessed Granny Edna's adventurous spirit, spreading joy to all who crossed her path.

Granny Edna's treasure hunt didn't end that day. It became a daily ritual, where she would embark on new quests and rediscover the wonders of her own life. Her forgetfulness became a mere whisper in the wind, overshadowed by the vibrant spirit that radiated from within.

Through her playful escapades, Granny Edna reminded everyone that age was just a number and that the true treasure of life lies in embracing each moment with childlike wonder. She inspired others to seek the hidden gems within their own lives and to never stop exploring, even when the world seemed unfamiliar.

And so, Granny Edna continued her adventures, weaving tales of joy and discovery wherever she went. Her zest for life and her unwavering spirit became a beacon of inspiration for all who crossed her path, leaving a trail of laughter and love in her wake.

The Nutty Surprise: Grandma's Delicious Discovery

In the cozy village of Oakridge, there lived a sweet and spirited grandmother named Evelyn. She had always been a picky eater, dismissing certain foods without giving them a chance. Among her long list of culinary dislikes were nuts, which she believed had no place in her palate.

Evelyn's granddaughter, Sophie, adored her grandma and wanted to expand her culinary horizons. She decided to introduce Evelyn to the world of nuts, hoping to change her perception. With a mischievous twinkle in her eye, Sophie devised a plan to surprise her grandma.

One sunny afternoon, Sophie prepared a batch of freshly roasted almonds, coating them with a hint of cinnamon and a sprinkle of sea salt. She presented the bowl of nuts to Evelyn, who eyed them hesitantly.

Curiosity got the better of Evelyn, and she cautiously picked up an almond, nibbling on it tentatively. As the nut crunched between her teeth, a burst of flavor exploded in her mouth. Her eyes widened, and a smile crept across her face. She had never expected nuts to be so delicious!

From that moment on, Evelyn's perspective shifted, and she eagerly embraced the world of nuts. Cashews, walnuts, and pistachios became her newfound companions. She marveled at their textures and savored their unique flavors.

Evelyn and Sophie spent countless afternoons experimenting with nut-based recipes, from creamy pesto to crunchy granola. They laughed and bonded over their shared love for these newfound culinary delights, creating cherished memories in the kitchen.

Word of Evelyn's nutty transformation spread throughout Oakridge, inspiring others to challenge their preconceived notions about food. Her story reminded the townspeople that it's never too late to explore new flavors and expand their culinary horizons.

Evelyn's newfound appreciation for nuts became a symbol of open-mindedness and the joy of discovery. She encouraged her friends and neighbors to embrace the unexpected, reminding them that sometimes the most delightful surprises come in the form of a humble nut.

Brushes of Dreams: Embracing Passion at Any Age

In the quiet town of Serenity Springs, there lived an elderly woman named Clara. Despite the passage of time, Clara's spirit remained youthful, and she harbored a secret dream within her heart.

For years, Clara had dreamed of becoming an artist. Every day, she would gaze at the vibrant paintings adorning her walls, longing to create her own masterpieces. Doubts often clouded her mind, whispering that it was too late to pursue her artistic aspirations.

One sunny morning, Clara stumbled upon an art class flyer at the local community center. Her heart fluttered with excitement and trepidation. With a surge of determination, she enrolled in the class, determined to breathe life into her dream.

Weeks turned into months as Clara immersed herself in the world of brushes and canvases. She discovered a newfound sense of joy and purpose as her artistic skills blossomed. Her paintings became a reflection of her vibrant spirit, each stroke telling a story of resilience and courage.

As word spread of Clara's artistic journey, the townspeople marveled at her talent and admired her unwavering pursuit of a dream. Clara's story became an inspiration to those who believed that age should never hinder the pursuit of passion.

In Serenity Springs, Clara's paintings adorned gallery walls, captivating the hearts of art enthusiasts far and wide. Her journey became a symbol of the indomitable human spirit and a testament to the power of following one's dreams.

Clara's story touched the lives of countless individuals, reminding them that it is never too late to embrace their passions and chase their dreams. Her journey inspired others to take bold steps towards their aspirations, no matter their age or circumstances.

Clara and the Mysterious Corn Disappearance

Once upon a time in the quiet village of Featherwing, Clara, the curious chicken, decided to embark on a new adventure. She woke up with a special feeling, as if something exciting was about to happen. Unable to resist the allure of mysteries, Clara's gaze fell upon the cornfield that stretched beyond her yard.

Being an inquisitive explorer, Clara set out to investigate this enigmatic green expanse. She ventured into the field, where she had never dared to tread before, and was amazed by the sight of lush, towering cornstalks. Each row held a new adventure for her.

But suddenly, Clara noticed something strange. All the juicy corn cobs were gone! Who could have stolen this delicious temptation? Clara decided to become a detective and solve the mystery.

Clara began her investigation, questioning the other animals around. They claimed to know nothing about the missing corn, but some had a suspicious twinkle in their eyes. Undeterred, Clara continued to search for clues.

And then, one day, Clara stumbled upon some tracks. She discovered corn husks leading to the barn. Clara thought that perhaps one of the animals had decided to make a winter stash.

With a heart full of determination, Clara opened the barn doors and... found her friend, Roger, the eloquent and nimble white rabbit. He was sitting on a pile of corn cobs, filled with mischievous satisfaction.

«Roger! Did you steal all the corn?» Clara exclaimed.

Roger confessed to his naughty escapade, laughing and apologizing at the same time. He explained how he couldn't resist the temptation when he saw the corn supply.

Clara sighed with relief and started laughing. They both knew it was a funny story, and no harm was done. In the end, they shared their spoils, relishing the juicy corn kernels together.

Clara and Roger became inseparable friends, sharing many adventures and laughter. And the cornfield became their special place, where they spent time together, enjoying nature and friendship.

The Laughter Within: Embracing Life's Whimsy with Henry

In a small cottage nestled by a glistening lake, lived a remarkable old man named Henry. Despite his battle with dementia, Henry possessed an unwavering spirit and a mischievous sense of humor that lit up the lives of those around him.

Every day, Henry would embark on whimsical adventures within the labyrinth of his own mind. His memories danced like fireflies, flickering in and out of reach. But instead of succumbing to frustration, Henry embraced the unpredictable nature of his thoughts and transformed them into laughter.

One sunny morning, as Henry sat in his favorite rocking chair, his mind wandered to the days of his youth. He chuckled, realizing he had forgotten where he had placed his glasses. With a twinkle in his eye, he declared, «Who needs glasses when life is a blur of excitement!»

His family, who had gathered around him, laughed along, appreciating Henry's ability to find joy even in moments of forgetfulness. They joined him in the search, playfully pretending to wear invisible glasses, bumping into walls and giggling uncontrollably.

Henry's charming wit extended to his encounters with others. He would greet friends and strangers alike with a mischievous smile, introducing himself as the «Grand Wizard of Forgetfulness» or the «Master of the Memory Maze.»

His infectious laughter turned encounters into whimsical encounters, leaving people with smiles that lasted long after the conversation had ended.

In the evenings, as the sun dipped below the horizon, Henry would gather with his loved ones around the fireplace. They would share stories, weaving together fragments of forgotten memories and imaginative tales. Henry's quick wit and comedic timing transformed these gatherings into magical moments, where laughter became the glue that held them all together.

Despite the challenges posed by his condition, Henry taught his family and friends invaluable lessons about resilience and finding joy in the face of adversity. He reminded them that life's journey was not always about remembering every detail, but rather about cherishing the connections and shared laughter that could never be forgotten.

As the years passed, Henry's legacy grew. His infectious laughter echoed through the walls of the cottage, bringing comfort to those who walked in his footsteps. His ability to transform his own forgetfulness into lighthearted jests became an inspiration to others facing similar challenges.

Henry, the unforgettable jester, reminded everyone that humor had the power to bridge the gap between the present and the past. His indomitable spirit touched the hearts of all who knew him, leaving an enduring legacy of laughter, love, and resilience.

A Slice of Laughter: The Apple Pie Adventure

In a cozy town, lifelong friends Emily and Sarah shared an unbreakable bond, filled with laughter and cherished memories. On a sunny day, Emily visited Sarah, intending to surprise her with a treasured family apple pie recipe. But to her dismay, she realized she had forgotten the recipe, arriving with only a bag of apples in hand.

Rather than succumbing to frustration, Emily's face lit up with a mischievous smile. She burst into laughter, unable to contain her amusement, and Sarah soon joined in, their giggles echoing through the house.

Embracing the unexpected turn of events, Emily suggested creating a new recipe together. With excitement in their eyes, they adorned matching aprons and dove into the adventure of making an apple pie from scratch.

Amidst peeling, slicing, and mixing, they reveled in their shared creativity, playfully tossing flour and swapping amusing stories. The kitchen transformed into a lively haven of joy and camaraderie.

As the homemade pie baked in the oven, anticipation swelled within them. The aroma wafting through the house was intoxicating, filling the air with the promise of a delectable treat.

When the timer chimed, Emily and Sarah carefully removed the golden pie from the oven. It may not have followed a precise recipe, but its appearance was mouthwatering. They eagerly served themselves slices, anticipation brimming in their eyes.

With the first taste, their faces lit up in delight. The pie was a symphony of flavors, a delightful blend of sweet and tangy. It may not have been the traditional family recipe, but it held the essence of their friendship, their laughter, and their ability to find joy in unforeseen circumstances.

They savored each bite, savoring the bond that had only grown stronger through their shared adventure.

From that day onward, the apple pie mishap became a cherished tale, a testament to their enduring friendship and the beauty of creating memories in the most unexpected ways.

Emily and Sarah continued to share laughter, mishaps, and heartwarming moments, reminding everyone around them that sometimes the sweetest moments in life emerge from the most amusing mistakes. Their friendship became a beacon of light, radiating joy and inspiring others to embrace the unexpected with open hearts and laughter on their lips.

The Joyful Game with a Furry Friend

As I stroll down the street, a burst of movement catches my eye—a small, fluffy cat happily playing with a vibrant red ribbon. It leaps, rolls, and twirls around the ribbon, as if discovering a world of endless amusement. Unable to resist, I approach the adorable sight, curious to join in the feline's playful escapade.

With a swift jump, the cat wraps itself around my legs, inviting me into the game. I can't help but comply, reaching into my pocket to reveal another ribbon. Tossing it into the air, the cat eagerly bounds after it, swatting and pouncing with grace and agility.

With each toss, the cat's enthusiasm grows, captivating my heart with its joyful energy. It's a delightful sight to behold as the furry companion jumps, twists, and performs acrobatic tricks to catch the elusive ribbon.

The game continues, and I am mesmerized by the pure happiness emanating from this simple interaction. The laughter that fills the air bridges the gap between species, forging a connection built on shared amusement.

As the last ribbon is presented to the cat, it expresses its gratitude by rubbing against my leg and purring contentedly. In that moment, a warmth envelops my heart, realizing that this impromptu game has brought genuine joy to both the cat and me.

This encounter serves as a poignant reminder of the power of play and lighthearted moments. It teaches me that even in the most unexpected times, laughter and games can brighten our lives, offering respite from any challenges we may face.

From that day forward, the memory of this delightful game with the cat remains etched in my mind—a constant reminder to seek joy, embrace playfulness, and find solace in the simplest of pleasures.

The Magical Painting Adventure

Have you ever imagined stepping into a painting and exploring a world of vibrant colors and enchanting landscapes? Well, let me take you on a whimsical journey through «The Magical Painting Adventure.»

One day, Alice, a curious and imaginative young girl, discovered a dusty old painting tucked away in the attic. As she stared at the picture, she couldn't help but wonder what it would be like to enter that mesmerizing scene.

With a mischievous grin, Alice took a deep breath and stepped right into the painting. To her amazement, she found herself in a breathtaking countryside filled with rolling hills, blooming flowers, and talking animals.

As Alice ventured further, she encountered a wise old owl perched on a branch. The owl, named Oliver, offered to be her guide through this extraordinary world. Together, they embarked on a quest to bring color and joy to the once-muted land.

Their first stop was the Painted Forest, where the trees stood in various shades of gray. Armed with a magical paintbrush, Alice carefully stroked each tree, turning them into a dazzling array of colors. The forest came alive with vibrant greens, blues, and pinks, and the animals who called it home rejoiced with glee.

Next, they arrived at the Silent Lake, where the water lay still and colorless.

With a playful flick of her brush, Alice created ripples of colors, transforming the lake into a shimmering masterpiece. Suddenly, the lake echoed with the joyful laughter of dancing water nymphs.

Their final destination was the Flower Meadow, where the flowers drooped with sadness. Alice tenderly painted each petal, infusing them with radiant hues. The flowers stretched towards the sky, swaying with newfound energy and releasing a sweet fragrance that filled the air.

As Alice and Oliver completed their colorful quest, the entire painted world sparkled with life and happiness. The once-dull painting had transformed into a vibrant realm of beauty and wonder.

With a grateful smile, Alice bid farewell to her newfound friends and stepped back into the real world. But the magic of «The Magical Painting Adventure» stayed with her forever, reminding her that a touch of color and imagination could transform even the gloomiest of days.

And so, Alice continued to explore the wonders of the world, always carrying the memory of her extraordinary journey within her heart.

The Timeless Dream

In a quiet town, there lived a gentle soul named Arthur. As a young boy, Arthur had dreams of becoming a painter, creating vibrant masterpieces that would capture the beauty of the world. But as life unfolded, responsibilities and obligations took precedence, and his dream slowly faded away.

Years passed, and Arthur found himself in his twilight years, reflecting on the path he had taken. He couldn't help but feel a sense of longing for the dreams he had let go.

One fateful day, while strolling through an art gallery, Arthur stumbled upon a painting that stirred something deep within him. The vibrant colors and exquisite brushstrokes transported him back to his childhood, rekindling the flame of his artistic aspirations.

In that moment, Arthur made a decision – it was never too late to chase his dreams. He dusted off his paintbrushes, gathered his paints, and set up a small studio in the corner of his living room.

At first, the strokes were hesitant and uncertain, but with each stroke, Arthur rediscovered the joy and passion that had once fueled his artistic spirit. He spent hours lost in the creative process, allowing his imagination to guide his hand.

As the days turned into weeks, Arthur's paintings began to take shape.

Each canvas was a testament to his newfound determination and the unwavering belief that it was never too late to pursue one's dreams.

Word of Arthur's talent spread throughout the town, and soon, his paintings were displayed in local galleries. People marveled at the beauty and emotion captured in his artwork, recognizing the depth and wisdom that only years of life experience could bring.

Arthur's journey inspired others, reminding them that age should never be a barrier to pursuing dreams. People began to revisit their own forgotten aspirations, reigniting their passions and embarking on new adventures.

As time went on, Arthur's artwork gained recognition far beyond the town's borders. His paintings found homes in prestigious galleries around the world, touching the hearts of countless individuals who, like him, had once let their dreams fade away.

With every stroke of his brush, Arthur proved that dreams were not bound by time. They were timeless, waiting patiently for us to reclaim them and bring them to life.

And so, the story of Arthur became a testament to the indomitable human spirit, reminding us that no matter how many years have passed, it is never too late to embrace our dreams, to chase our passions, and to fill our lives with the colors that make our souls come alive.

The Pancake Mishap: A Recipe for Laughter

Let me share with you the uproarious tale of «The Pancake Mishap,» where a seemingly ordinary pancake recipe takes a hilarious turn.

One sunny morning, Grandma Edith decided to pass down the secret family recipe for the most mouthwatering pancakes to her granddaughter, Lily. Flour filled the air, and the sweet scent of vanilla wafted through the kitchen as they embarked on their culinary adventure.

Grandma Edith carefully measured the flour, sugar, and baking powder into a mixing bowl. As she reached for the salt, she turned to Lily and said, «Now, my dear, the most important ingredient: the milk!»

With a mischievous grin, Lily handed her the milk carton. Unbeknownst to them, it was empty, setting the stage for a pancake fiasco.

Grandma poured the imaginary milk into the bowl and started stirring the batter. As they chatted and mixed, confusion clouded Grandma Edith's face. She glanced at Lily and asked, «Why isn't the batter turning out right? It's supposed to be runny!»

Both perplexed, Lily scratched her head until it hit them like a pancake flipping mid-air—they had forgotten to add the milk!

Laughter erupted as they realized their mishap was caused by an empty carton.

Amidst their giggles, Grandma Edith proclaimed, «Well, Lily, it seems we've created our own special pancake recipe—the world's first 'Dry Batter Pancakes'!» They chuckled at the absurdity of their blunder.

Determined not to let their mishap go to waste, Grandma heated the griddle, dropping spoonfuls of the thick batter onto the hot surface. The pancakes sizzled, taking on a peculiar shade of brown, but their spirits remained high.

When it was time to taste their unconventional creation, Lily spread butter on her pancake, while Grandma Edith poured syrup with a mischievous twinkle in her eye. The first bites revealed unexpectedly delightful results—crispy exteriors and surprisingly fluffy interiors.

With each bite, their laughter grew louder as they marveled at their unintentional culinary invention. They had stumbled upon a new pancake variation, forever known as «The Dry Batter Delight.»

From that day forward, Lily and Grandma Edith cherished their unique pancake mishap, turning it into a beloved family tradition. The laughter and memories shared over their «Dry Batter Delight» pancakes served as a reminder that the best moments in life often arise from unexpected twists and turns.

The Grandson's Mischievous Scare

One sunny afternoon, young Tommy visited his grandfather, affectionately known as Grandpa Joe. Tommy was always full of playful tricks and mischievous antics, and this day was no exception.

As Grandpa Joe sat peacefully on his favorite rocking chair, engrossed in a crossword puzzle, Tommy tiptoed behind him, plotting a playful scare. With a sly grin on his face, Tommy let out a sudden, loud «Boo!»

Startled, Grandpa Joe's crossword puzzle flew into the air, and he let out a surprised yelp. But within seconds, he realized it was his mischievous grandson responsible for the scare.

Grandpa Joe couldn't help but burst into laughter, his deep belly laugh filling the room. Tommy joined in, their laughter intertwining, creating a symphony of joy and amusement.

Grandpa Joe, wiping away tears of laughter, said, «Oh, you got me good, Tommy! I thought there was a ghost sneaking up on me.»

Tommy, beaming with pride, replied, «I couldn't resist, Grandpa! You're always so calm and collected. I wanted to see your funny reaction.»

From that day on, the scare became a cherished memory between Grandpa Joe and Tommy.

It became a delightful inside joke, a reminder of their bond and the shared laughter that filled their hearts.

As the years went by, Tommy continued to surprise Grandpa Joe with his playful pranks, and each time, their laughter grew louder and their bond stronger. They cherished those moments, knowing that the joy they found in each other's company was a precious gift.

The story of the grandson's mischievous scare became legendary in their family. It was retold at family gatherings and filled with laughter, reminding everyone of the importance of playfulness and the enduring power of laughter.

And so, Grandpa Joe and Tommy taught their family that even in the simplest moments, a mischievous scare could ignite laughter and create a lasting connection. Their shared laughter became a symbol of love, joy, and the beautiful bond between a grandfather and his mischievous grandson.

The Unforgettable Dance

In the vibrant community of Silver Springs Retirement Village, where friendship blossomed like wildflowers, lived a group of spirited seniors who knew how to make each day an adventure. Among them was Evelyn, a vivacious and free-spirited lady who had a zest for life and an infectious laughter that could brighten even the gloomiest of days.

One sunny afternoon, as the residents gathered for their weekly dance session, Evelyn couldn't contain her excitement. Music filled the air, and the sound of lively chatter echoed throughout the room. As the first notes of a lively foxtrot played, Evelyn's eyes sparkled with anticipation.

But as Evelyn stepped onto the dance floor, she realized something was amiss. Her beloved dance partner, Jack, was nowhere to be found. The disappointment weighed heavy on her heart, as she had been eagerly looking forward to twirling and spinning around the dance floor with him.

Undeterred by the setback, Evelyn decided to take matters into her own hands. With a mischievous glimmer in her eye, she turned to her friend, Margaret, and asked, «Margaret, my dear, have you ever waltzed with a broomstick as your partner?»

Margaret couldn't help but chuckle at Evelyn's playful suggestion. «Oh, Evelyn, you always know how to bring a smile to our faces! But dancing with a broomstick? That's a new one. I'm game if you are!»

With their spirits high, Evelyn and Margaret grabbed a broomstick each and took to the dance floor. They twirled, dipped, and laughed their way through the foxtrot, their improvised partners adding an extra element of hilarity to their moves.

The room erupted in applause and laughter as the residents watched Evelyn and Margaret sweep across the dance floor, their carefree and lighthearted dance captivating everyone's hearts. They celebrated the joy of the moment, embracing the freedom to be silly and the beauty of friendship.

As the music faded and Evelyn and Margaret took their final bow, the room echoed with cheers and applause. The memory of their unforgettable dance became a legendary tale in the retirement village, a reminder that age was never a barrier to joy and laughter.

From that day forward, Evelyn and Margaret became the dynamic duo of Silver Springs Retirement Village, always finding ways to infuse laughter and merriment into their daily lives. They continued to create cherished memories, reminding their friends that life was meant to be lived with gusto, no matter the circumstances.

The story of «The Unforgettable Dance» brought a smile to the faces of the residents, inspiring them to embrace spontaneity, find joy in the simplest moments, and let their spirits dance freely, just like Evelyn and Margaret.

The Hilarious Fishing Expedition

In the quaint fishing village of Seabreeze Bay, there resided a group of lively retirees who loved nothing more than casting their lines into the sparkling waters in search of the day's catch. Among them was George, a jolly old man with a knack for fishing and a mischievous sense of humor.

One fine morning, George and his fishing buddies gathered at the pier, their fishing gear in hand and anticipation in their eyes. As they set sail on their small boats, the salty breeze filled their lungs with excitement.

As the hours passed by, the fishermen exchanged stories and laughter, enjoying the camaraderie that came with their shared passion. But amidst the banter, George couldn't resist playing a prank on his unsuspecting friends.

With a twinkle in his eye, George pretended to have caught the biggest fish of the day. He tugged on his fishing rod, feigning a mighty struggle, and exclaimed, «I've got a whopper here, boys!»

His friends, eager to witness George's triumph, rushed to his side, offering encouragement and readying their nets. But as George reeled in his «prize,» a burst of laughter erupted from his mischievous lips. Instead of a magnificent fish, he held up a comically large rubber boot that he had cunningly attached to his line.

The fishermen roared with laughter, their eyes crinkling with joy. They couldn't help but admire George's clever prank, appreciating his ability to inject humor into their fishing expedition. The rubber boot became a symbol of their shared laughter and camaraderie.

As the boats returned to the shore, George proudly displayed his «catch» to the other villagers who had gathered to witness their return. The sight of George triumphantly hoisting the rubber boot elicited a chorus of laughter that echoed throughout Seabreeze Bay.

From that day forward, the fishing village lovingly referred to the incident as «The Hilarious Fishing Expedition,» a tale that became legendary among the locals. It reminded them that life was meant to be enjoyed, even in the simplest of moments, and that laughter had the power to create lasting bonds.

The story of «The Hilarious Fishing Expedition» spread beyond Seabreeze Bay, bringing smiles to the faces of all who heard it. It served as a reminder to embrace the lighter side of life, to appreciate the joy in shared laughter, and to treasure the memories made with cherished friends.

From Skeptic to Savory: Grandpa's Journey to Healthy Eating

In the cozy town of Harmony Hills, there lived a spirited old man named Henry. He was known for his love of hearty meals, indulging in rich flavors and savory delights. But as the years went by, Henry's health began to decline, and his family grew concerned.

One day, Henry's granddaughter, Lily, introduced him to the concept of healthy eating. She explained the benefits of nourishing his body with wholesome foods and how it could improve his overall well-being. Skeptical at first, Henry couldn't fathom a meal without his beloved comfort foods.

However, Lily was determined to change her grandpa's perspective. She started by preparing nutritious meals that were as delicious as they were nourishing. With each bite, Henry discovered a world of flavors he had never imagined.

Lily incorporated fresh fruits, vegetables, and whole grains into their meals, proving that healthy eating didn't mean sacrificing taste. Henry's taste buds awakened to the vibrant flavors and textures of his new culinary adventures.

As weeks turned into months, Henry's health began to improve. He had more energy, felt lighter, and even shed a few pounds. The transformation amazed him, and he realized that healthy eating could be a source of joy and vitality.

Embracing his newfound appreciation for wholesome cuisine, Henry eagerly joined Lily in exploring new recipes and experimenting with nutritious ingredients. They laughed and bonded over their culinary adventures, savoring the delights they created together.

The aroma of nourishing meals filled Henry's home, and the townspeople couldn't help but be intrigued. Henry's journey to healthy eating inspired others to reevaluate their own dietary choices, proving that one could find satisfaction in mindful consumption.

In Harmony Hills, Henry became a symbol of the power of change and the joys of embracing a healthier lifestyle. His story inspired the community to prioritize their well-being, nourishing both body and soul through the food they consumed.

The Whistling Teapot

Have you ever encountered an object that seemed to have a mind of its own? Let me share with you the delightful tale of Mrs. Thompson and her mischievous teapot.

Mrs. Thompson was an avid tea drinker who cherished her daily ritual of brewing a warm cup of tea. One day, she brought home a new teapot with a unique quirk – it had a tendency to whistle at the most unexpected moments.

As Mrs. Thompson filled the teapot with water and placed it on the stove, she couldn't help but wonder what surprises awaited her. Sure enough, as the water reached its boiling point, the teapot let out a loud, melodic whistle that echoed throughout the kitchen.

Amused by the unexpected symphony, Mrs. Thompson couldn't resist giggling at the teapot's lively personality. From that day forward, every time she made tea, she eagerly awaited the whimsical whistle.

Word spread quickly about Mrs. Thompson's whistling teapot, and soon friends and neighbors would gather in her kitchen just to witness the delightful spectacle. They would exchange stories and laughter, all while savoring the comforting aroma of freshly brewed tea.

The teapot seemed to have a mischievous charm, turning ordinary tea time into a lively and memorable experience.

It brought people together, fostering a sense of joy and camaraderie that warmed their hearts.

As the years went by, Mrs. Thompson's teapot became a cherished symbol of friendship and shared laughter. It became a tradition for guests to bring their favorite tea leaves, eager to hear the whimsical whistle and create lasting memories.

The whistling teapot taught Mrs. Thompson an important lesson – sometimes, it's the unexpected quirks and surprises in life that bring us the most joy. It reminded her to embrace the spontaneity and find humor in the everyday moments, transforming them into cherished memories.

So, the next time you enjoy a cup of tea, remember the tale of Mrs. Thompson and her mischievous teapot. Embrace the unexpected melodies that life brings, gather your loved ones, and let laughter fill the air as you create your own magical moments.

The Mysterious Case of the Vanishing Cookies

In a cozy kitchen nestled in a small town, Grandma Agnes was known for her delectable homemade cookies. One day, as she busily prepared a batch of her famous chocolate chip cookies, her mischievous granddaughter, Lucy, couldn't resist the temptation. While Grandma's back was turned, Lucy sneaked into the kitchen and snatched a handful of freshly baked cookies.

Unaware of Lucy's sneaky maneuver, Grandma Agnes turned around to find her cookies mysteriously missing. She scratched her head, trying to recall where she had placed them. Lucy, with a mischievous grin, innocently asked, «Grandma, have you looked under the oven? Maybe they rolled away!»

As Grandma Agnes stooped down to check under the oven, she burst into laughter. There, hidden in a clever hiding spot, were the missing cookies. Lucy's quick thinking had created a delightful moment of mischief and laughter.

From that day forward, whenever Grandma Agnes baked cookies, Lucy would playfully remind her to keep an eye on the mischievous cookie thief. It became a cherished tradition, filled with laughter and warm memories. And as Grandma Agnes and Lucy shared their freshly baked treats, they couldn't help but savor the sweet taste of love and mischief that filled their hearts.

In that little kitchen, the mystery of the vanishing cookies brought joy and laughter, reminding Grandma Agnes and Lucy that even in the face of small mishaps, life was always sweeter with a mischievous twist.

The Gift of a Second Chance

In a bustling city filled with dreams and aspirations, there lived a woman named Emily. She was a beacon of resilience and determination, despite the challenges life had thrown her way. Emily had always harbored a deep passion for painting, but circumstances had kept her dreams confined to the corners of her heart.

One day, as fate would have it, Emily stumbled upon an old, forgotten art studio. It stood with peeling paint and cracked windows, longing for a second chance, just like her. Inspired by the neglected beauty, Emily mustered the courage to lease the space and revive it.

With paintbrush in hand and a heart full of hope, Emily transformed the derelict studio into a vibrant sanctuary of art. She filled the walls with colorful strokes and breathed life into forgotten canvases. As word of her reimagined studio spread, curious souls flocked to witness the magic unfolding within those once-desolate walls.

Emily's newfound purpose touched the hearts of aspiring artists who had abandoned their own creative dreams. One by one, they joined her in the studio, brushing off their doubts and rekindling their passion for art. Guided by Emily's unwavering belief in their potential, they dared to dream once again.

Together, they created a nurturing community, where inspiration flowed freely, and self-expression flourished.

The once-silent studio echoed with laughter, stories, and shared artistic journeys. Bound by a common desire to embrace their talents, they became each other's cheerleaders, providing the support and encouragement needed to grow.

As years passed, Emily's studio transformed into a vibrant hub of artistic expression, touching the lives of countless individuals. The walls, once dull and lifeless, now showcased a tapestry of stories told through strokes of paint. Each brushstroke spoke of courage, resilience, and the indomitable spirit of chasing dreams.

Emily's legacy extended beyond the walls of her studio. Her story became an inspiration for those who had shelved their passions, reminding them that it is never too late to pursue their dreams. Her journey ignited a spark within their souls, urging them to seize every moment and embrace their innate talents.

And so, in the heart of that bustling city, Emily's art studio became a haven for dreamers, a sanctuary where second chances were embraced, and creativity flourished. It stood as a testament to the transformative power of following one's passion and the extraordinary heights that can be reached when we believe in ourselves.

In the footsteps of Emily, countless individuals dared to pick up the brush, giving life to their dreams and painting their own extraordinary stories on the canvas of life.

Grandma's Hilarious Yoga Journey

Once upon a time, in a peaceful neighborhood, lived a spirited grandmother named Martha. Martha was known for her zest for life and her desire to try new things. One day, she decided to embark on a yoga adventure and, much to everyone's surprise, she convinced her husband, Harold, to join her.

With yoga mats in hand and open minds, Martha and Harold entered the serene yoga studio. As they found their spots among the other participants, their excitement mixed with a hint of nervous anticipation.

The instructor, a serene and flexible yoga guru named Maya, welcomed the class and began guiding them through a series of poses. Martha, eager to immerse herself in the practice, enthusiastically followed Maya's instructions. Harold, on the other hand, struggled to keep up with the fluid movements.

As the class progressed, Martha gracefully transitioned from one pose to another, bending and stretching with ease. Harold, on the other hand, found himself tangled in his yoga mat, inadvertently bumping into his neighbors, and occasionally toppling over in the most amusing positions.

Each time Harold stumbled, Martha couldn't help but burst into uncontrollable laughter. The entire class joined in, finding joy in Harold's valiant attempts and unwavering determination. Maya, the instructor, offered gentle encouragement and adjusted Harold's poses, creating an atmosphere filled with warmth and support.

Despite the challenges, Harold persevered, his determination matched only by Martha's unwavering support. He laughed at himself, embracing the lightheartedness of the situation. With each stumble, he learned to find his balance, both physically and metaphorically.

The yoga class became a regular occurrence for Martha and Harold. They attended with a mix of anticipation and laughter, knowing that their yoga journey was not just about mastering poses but about cherishing the bond they shared.

Over time, Harold's yoga skills improved, and he surprised everyone with his newfound flexibility and grace. But even as he became more skilled, his lighthearted spirit remained, providing a source of laughter and inspiration to those around him.

Martha and Harold's yoga journey taught them valuable lessons beyond the physical practice. They learned to embrace vulnerability, find humor in life's mishaps, and support each other unconditionally. Their dedication to the practice and their unwavering laughter became an inspiration to their fellow yogis, fostering a sense of unity and joy within the studio.

As Martha and Harold continued their yoga adventure, their love for each other grew stronger, and their laughter echoed through their home and into the hearts of their children and grandchildren. Their playful spirit served as a reminder to never take life too seriously and to always find joy in the simplest of moments.

The Mischievous Legacy of Harold's Rubber Chicken Prank

In a quaint countryside town, resided the eccentric Harold, renowned for his mischievous humor and unique perspective on life. Despite his battles with dementia, Harold's wit remained intact. One sunny morning, he devised a playful plan to prank his neighbors, Mr. and Mrs. Johnson.

Harold carefully selected a squawking rubber chicken from his collection, attaching a fishing line to its leg. With a mischievous twinkle in his eye, he positioned himself on the front porch, ready to execute his scheme. A gentle tug on the line sent the chicken bouncing into the Johnsons' yard, seemingly alive.

Bewildered, Mr. and Mrs. Johnson approached the comical spectacle with caution, exchanging perplexed glances. Harold, struggling to contain his amusement, observed the scene unfold. His laughter grew as the chicken hopped and flopped, eventually bursting into uncontrollable giggles that reverberated through the neighborhood.

Realizing Harold's involvement, the Johnsons joined in the laughter, embracing the whimsy of the situation. This prank soon gained legendary status, with the townsfolk eagerly anticipating Harold's next humorous escapade.

As Harold's dementia progressed, his sense of humor remained a beacon of joy.

The rubber chicken became a symbol of his resilient spirit, reminding the community that laughter could brighten even the darkest days.

In that little town, filled with love and laughter, Harold's legacy thrived. His mischievous spirit bridged gaps, brought people together, and created cherished memories. Encountering a rubber chicken, residents couldn't help but smile, knowing Harold's pranks would continue to uplift their lives for years to come.

The Hilarious Misadventures of Grandpa and Grandson

Once upon a time, in a small town filled with laughter, there lived a mischievous grandpa named Harold and his energetic grandson, Max. Their days were always filled with laughter, silly antics, and unforgettable adventures.

One sunny morning, Grandpa Harold woke up with an ingenious plan. He decided to surprise Max with a homemade rocket launch in the backyard. Armed with a cardboard box, colorful paper, and a whole lot of imagination, Grandpa set to work on their rocket creation.

With paintbrushes in hand, they transformed the cardboard box into a magnificent spaceship, complete with buttons, levers, and even a makeshift control panel. Grandpa Harold was convinced it would take them to the moon and back!

Excitement filled the air as the duo prepared for the grand launch. They put on their astronaut helmets (which were actually just modified kitchen pots) and counted down from ten, eagerly anticipating their intergalactic adventure.

As the countdown reached zero, Grandpa Harold ignited the rocket engines. But instead of soaring high into the sky, the rocket sputtered, shook, and promptly tipped over. To their surprise, they found themselves crash-landing right into a giant pile of freshly raked leaves!

Laughter erupted from both of them as they emerged from the leafy wreckage, covered from head to toe in autumn hues. They had unintentionally created the most hilarious leaf pile landing in the history of rocket launches!

Undeterred by the failed launch, Grandpa Harold and Max turned the mishap into an opportunity for more laughter. They embraced their leafy camouflage and engaged in an epic leaf fight, tossing colorful leaves at each other and rolling around in the leafy madness.

Passersby couldn't help but join in the laughter and cheer as they witnessed the extraordinary sight of a grandpa and grandson frolicking in a sea of leaves. The entire neighborhood became a playground of joy, and even the squirrels joined the leafy chaos, darting in and out of the pile.

Eventually, exhaustion took hold, and they collapsed into the leaf pile, giggling and catching their breath. Covered head to toe in leaves, Grandpa Harold and Max shared a moment of pure happiness and contentment.

As they headed back inside, leaving behind the leafy battlefield, they left a trail of laughter and joy behind them. The memory of their hilarious misadventure would forever be cherished in their hearts and would become a legendary tale passed down through generations.

The Yarn-Filled Shenanigans

In a cozy little cottage, nestled amidst a colorful garden, lived Grandma Margaret, a knitting enthusiast, and her mischievous feline companion, Mr. Whiskers. Together, they shared an amusing tale that would tickle the hearts of all who heard it.

Grandma Margaret had a passion for knitting. With nimble fingers and a creative mind, she would spend hours transforming balls of yarn into beautiful creations. Her cozy blankets and warm sweaters were the talk of the town.

One sunny afternoon, as Grandma Margaret settled into her favorite armchair, her knitting needles poised for action, Mr. Whiskers sauntered into the room, his eyes gleaming mischievously. In his paws, he clutched a tantalizing ball of yarn.

As Grandma Margaret immersed herself in her knitting project, Mr. Whiskers seized the opportunity for a playful adventure. With a flick of his paw, he sent the ball of yarn rolling across the room, leaving a trail of tangled mischief in its wake.

Unaware of Mr. Whiskers' shenanigans, Grandma Margaret continued knitting, occasionally glancing over at the mischievous feline. But as the minutes ticked by, she noticed something peculiar – her ball of yarn was gradually disappearing.

Perplexed, Grandma Margaret searched high and low, unraveling a tangled mess of yarn across the room.

She followed the thread, which led her to Mr. Whiskers, gleefully playing with the last remnants of the ball of yarn.

Their eyes met, and Grandma Margaret couldn't help but burst into laughter. «Oh, Mr. Whiskers! You've turned my knitting room into a yarny playground! I hope you've had as much fun as I've had chasing after you.»

Mr. Whiskers purred in response, his tail flicking with delight, as if he understood Grandma Margaret's words.

With a mischievous twinkle in her eyes, Grandma Margaret set aside her knitting needles and decided to join Mr. Whiskers in his yarn-filled escapade. Together, they embraced the delightful chaos, twirling in loops of yarn and creating a whimsical masterpiece of tangled threads.

As they danced amidst the yarn, laughter filled the air, and the room became a haven of joy and shared merriment. Their playful bond grew stronger, and the memory of their yarn-filled adventure became a cherished tale in their household.

From that day forward, Grandma Margaret and Mr. Whiskers continued their playful escapades. Their yarn-filled antics brought laughter not only to their home but also to the hearts of all who heard their delightful tale.

The Forgetful Reminder

Have you ever had a little reminder that helped you remember something important? Let me share with you a heartwarming story about Mr. Johnson and his forgetful nature when it came to taking his medication.

Mr. Johnson was a kind-hearted gentleman who believed in the power of routine. Every day, he diligently took his medication to maintain his health. However, there was one small problem – he often forgot to take his pills on time.

One day, his caring granddaughter, Lily, decided to take matters into her own hands. She gifted him a colorful pillbox with compartments for each day of the week. With a mischievous smile, she said, «Grandpa, now you won't forget to take your pills!»

Mr. Johnson chuckled, appreciating Lily's thoughtful gesture. Little did he know that the pillbox would become much more than just a reminder.

Every morning, as Mr. Johnson opened the pillbox, he was greeted by a surprise. Lily had placed small handwritten notes inside each compartment. They were filled with words of encouragement, silly jokes, and reminders of their shared memories.

As Mr. Johnson read the notes, a smile would spread across his face.

Each message brought warmth to his heart, and he felt a renewed sense of connection with his granddaughter, even when she couldn't be by his side.

The pillbox became more than a tool for remembering medication; it became a symbol of love and support. It reminded Mr. Johnson that he was not alone in his journey and that someone cared deeply about his well-being.

With Lily's creative approach, taking medication became an enjoyable ritual. Mr. Johnson looked forward to opening each compartment, not only for the pills but also for the heartfelt notes that brightened his day.

The forgetful reminder brought Mr. Johnson and Lily closer together. They would often sit together, reminiscing about old times, sharing laughter, and discussing the new notes that Lily would carefully craft each week.

And so, in the heartwarming tale of Mr. Johnson and his forgetful reminder, we learn that even the simplest gestures can make a profound impact. Sometimes, all it takes is a little creativity, love, and understanding to turn a routine task into a cherished moment of connection.

So, the next time you encounter a forgetful moment, remember the story of Mr. Johnson and his pillbox filled with love. Embrace the power of small gestures and use them to brighten someone's day, making their journey a little lighter and their hearts a little happier.

The Mischievous Duo at the Senior Home

In a cozy senior home nestled amidst picturesque surroundings, two mischievous residents, Harold and Mildred, formed an unlikely duo. They were known for their playful antics and contagious laughter that echoed through the halls.

One sunny afternoon, Harold and Mildred found themselves engrossed in a friendly game of chess. As the game progressed, their competitive spirits ignited, and they strategized with mischievous glimmers in their eyes.

Harold, with a mischievous grin, plotted a clever move. He pretended to be deep in thought, stroking his chin, while his eyes darted to a nearby window. Seizing the opportunity, he secretly moved a pawn with lightning speed when Mildred wasn't looking.

Mildred, ever observant, noticed Harold's sly maneuver. She raised an eyebrow and countered with her own sneaky move, sliding her bishop across the board when Harold's attention was momentarily diverted.

The game continued with a series of unexpected twists and turns, each move accompanied by laughter and playful banter. The other residents gathered around, enjoying the lively spectacle and eagerly placing bets on who would emerge victorious.

As the game reached its climax, Mildred executed a daring move that took Harold by surprise. He burst into laughter, tipping his king over in mock surrender. The room erupted in applause and laughter, celebrating their spirited competition.

But their mischief didn't end there. With a twinkle in their eyes, Harold and Mildred decided to have a little fun with the staff. They pretended to argue over who would clean up the chessboard, creating a hilarious commotion that left the unsuspecting caregivers in fits of laughter.

Harold and Mildred's infectious joy spread throughout the senior home, brightening the spirits of all who crossed their path. Their playful antics reminded everyone that age was just a number and that life could still be full of laughter and adventure.

Their mischievous bond grew stronger with each passing day, as they continued to create moments of joy and mischief. Whether it was organizing impromptu dance parties or organizing secret treasure hunts, Harold and Mildred infused the senior home with a vibrant and lighthearted atmosphere.

Their legacy remained etched in the hearts of those who knew them, inspiring others to embrace the playful side of life, regardless of age. Harold and Mildred, the mischievous duo, taught everyone the power of laughter, camaraderie, and staying young at heart.

The Courageous Chicken

Have you ever heard a tale about a chicken that was braver than it appeared? Let me share with you a funny and inspiring story about a little hen named Henrietta.

Henrietta lived on a cozy farm with other farm animals, but she was often teased by her fellow chickens for being timid. She dreamed of being bold and courageous like the farm dog or the majestic horses.

One sunny morning, as Henrietta strutted around the farmyard, she noticed a commotion near the vegetable patch. A group of mischievous crows were swooping down, pecking at the newly planted seeds. The farm dog and the horses were too busy to notice, and the other chickens cowered in fear.

Feeling a surge of determination, Henrietta puffed up her feathers and bravely marched toward the crows. With each step, she clucked defiantly, as if to say, «Not today, you pesky crows!»

The crows, startled by Henrietta's unexpected courage, took to the skies, leaving the garden in peace. The other chickens watched in awe as Henrietta saved the day, her small size belying her tremendous bravery.

From that moment on, Henrietta became known as the «Courageous Chicken» of the farm.

She fearlessly defended her feathered friends, standing up to any challenges that came their way. The other chickens realized that bravery came in all shapes and sizes, and they too began to find their own inner courage.

Henrietta's act of bravery inspired the other animals on the farm. The horse galloped a little faster, the sheep stood a little taller, and even the farm dog wagged his tail with newfound confidence. Henrietta had shown them that it's not about the size of the chicken in the fight, but the size of the fight in the chicken.

And so, the tale of Henrietta, the Courageous Chicken, reminds us that courage can be found in the most unexpected places. It teaches us to embrace our fears, stand tall in the face of challenges, and inspire others with our bravery.

So, the next time you feel a bit timid or unsure, think of Henrietta and let her story remind you that courage knows no boundaries. Embrace your inner bravery, spread your wings, and face the world with a cluck of determination. After all, you never know how far your courage might take you.

Grandpa Friends: Fishing Adventure

Grandpas Max and Leo had been best friends for many years. They both loved spending time in the great outdoors, and their favorite activity was fishing. Every weekend, rain or shine, they would pack up their fishing gear and head to their favorite fishing spot by the lake.

One sunny morning, Grandpas Max and Leo set out on their usual fishing trip. They were excited to see who would catch the biggest fish that day. As they settled by the water, they couldn't help but reminisce about their past fishing adventures and share stories of the ones that got away.

After a few hours of patiently waiting, their fishing lines finally started to wiggle. They both jumped up in excitement, thinking they had caught something big. But to their surprise, their lines got tangled, and they ended up reeling in each other's lines instead.

They burst into laughter, realizing what had happened. Grandpa Max exclaimed, «Well, Leo, it seems we've caught each other instead of fish this time!» Grandpa Leo replied with a chuckle, «That's true, Max. We make a great team, even when it comes to catching each other's lines!»

They spent the rest of the day untangling their lines and sharing more laughter and stories.

Even though they didn't catch any fish that day, they realized that the best catch of all was the friendship they shared.

From that day on, Grandpas Max and Leo always looked forward to their fishing trips, not just for the chance to catch fish but also for the opportunity to create more cherished memories together.

And so, the adventures of the two grandpa friends continued, filled with laughter, fishing tales, and a bond that grew stronger with every fishing trip they took.

The Adventurous Grannies: A Joyful Journey

Once upon a time, in a cozy little village, there were two adventurous grannies named Ethel and Mildred. Despite their age, they were always full of energy and ready for new experiences. Together, they embarked on exciting escapades that left everyone amazed.

One sunny morning, Ethel and Mildred decided to go on a spontaneous road trip. They packed their suitcases, put on their favorite hats, and hopped into Mildred's trusty old car. With the wind in their hair and laughter in their hearts, they set off on a journey of a lifetime.

Their first stop was a quaint little town known for its delicious pastries. Ethel and Mildred couldn't resist the aroma of freshly baked goodies, so they decided to try every sweet treat in the bakery. With icing on their noses and crumbs on their cheeks, they giggled like schoolgirls, savoring each delectable bite.

Next, they ventured into the nearby forest for a nature hike. Armed with walking sticks and an adventurous spirit, they explored winding trails and discovered hidden treasures along the way. They marveled at the beauty of the trees, the songs of the birds, and the tranquility of nature that surrounded them.

But their adventure didn't end there. Ethel and Mildred were determined to conquer their fear of heights.

They found a hot air balloon festival nearby and eagerly signed up for a ride. As the balloon gently ascended into the sky, they held hands tightly and looked down at the world below. The breathtaking view erased their fears and filled their hearts with pure exhilaration.

Their journey was filled with laughter, joy, and countless memorable moments. Ethel and Mildred didn't let their age hold them back. They proved that life was meant to be lived to the fullest, regardless of how many candles adorned their birthday cakes.

As they returned home from their grand adventure, the village greeted them with open arms and wide smiles. Ethel and Mildred became an inspiration to everyone, showing that age was just a number and that the spirit of adventure never grows old.

From that day forward, the village celebrated the spirit of the adventurous grannies. They organized outdoor excursions, dance parties, and even a yearly hot air balloon festival in their honor. Ethel and Mildred continued to live life to the fullest, reminding everyone that it's never too late to embark on new adventures and create lasting memories.

So, if you ever come across a pair of adventurous grannies named Ethel and Mildred, be prepared to join in their joyful journey. Together, you'll discover the beauty of friendship, the thrill of exploration, and the timeless joy of living life to the fullest.

Blooming Memories: Grandma and Granddaughter's Floral Journey

In a quaint little cottage surrounded by a vibrant garden, lived a wise and gentle grandma named Rosemary, and her loving granddaughter, Emily. Their shared love for nature brought them closer together, creating a bond that blossomed with each passing day.

Grandma Rosemary had always been an avid gardener, with a vast collection of flowers blooming in her backyard. She knew every flower by name and could describe their colors, scents, and meanings with great detail. Her garden was her sanctuary, and she wanted to pass down her knowledge to her beloved granddaughter.

As Emily grew older, she spent countless hours with Grandma Rosemary in the garden, learning the names of each flower and marveling at their beauty. They would stroll through the rows of roses, tulips, daisies, and daffodils, Grandma sharing stories and folklore associated with each bloom.

But as the years passed, Grandma Rosemary's memory began to fade. The vibrant petals and names of the flowers she once cherished became elusive, slipping through the cracks of her mind. It was a difficult realization for both of them, but Emily was determined to help her grandma hold onto her precious memories.

With compassion and patience, Emily became Grandma Rosemary's guide through the garden. She would gently point to each flower, whispering its name, and encouraging her grandma to recall the details they had shared. Sometimes, they would laugh together as Grandma playfully came up with unique names for the flowers, turning a forgetful moment into a joyful one.

The garden became a canvas of love and resilience, where the colors and fragrances of the flowers intertwined with the bonds of their relationship. Each day, they would walk hand in hand, their voices filling the air with laughter and the sweet aroma of blossoms. It didn't matter if the names were forgotten; what mattered was the shared experience, the connection that transcended words.

As time went on, Emily noticed something beautiful happening. Though Grandma Rosemary's memory continued to fade, her love for the garden remained steadfast. She would sit on a bench, admiring the blooms, humming melodies of forgotten songs, and feeling a sense of peace that only nature could bring.

Emily realized that the garden had become their sanctuary, a place where memories were etched in the petals, where the colors spoke the unspoken, and where love flourished in the midst of forgetfulness. It was a testament to the power of connection and the resilience of the human spirit. In their garden of blooming memories, Grandma Rosemary and Emily found solace, strength, and the beauty of unconditional love.

The Mischievous Dentures

In a cozy retirement home filled with laughter and camaraderie, lived a group of lively seniors who were always up for a good chuckle. Among them was Harold, a mischievous and quick-witted gentleman who had a knack for turning everyday situations into comedic adventures.

One sunny afternoon, as the residents gathered in the common area, Harold couldn't help but notice his friend Martha struggling with something. Her dentures seemed to be giving her trouble, as she adjusted and readjusted them with a perplexed expression on her face.

Curiosity getting the better of him, Harold approached Martha with a playful grin. «Martha, my dear, have you ever lost your teeth while they were still in your mouth?»

Martha chuckled and replied, «Oh, Harold, you always have a way with words! But no, I haven't lost them. They just don't seem to fit right today. I can't seem to find a comfortable spot for them.»

A mischievous sparkle danced in Harold's eyes as he hatched a plan. With a theatrical flourish, he reached into his pocket and pulled out a pair of fake dentures he had purchased as a gag gift. «Martha, my dear, perhaps I have just the solution for you!»

Martha looked at the fake dentures, a mix of amusement and skepticism in her eyes.

«Oh, Harold, you're always up to some sort of mischief. What do you have in mind?»

Harold couldn't contain his laughter as he handed the fake dentures to Martha. «Why don't you give these a try? Who knows, they might bring you the comfort and confidence you're looking for.»

With a twinkle in her eye, Martha took the fake dentures and cautiously placed them in her mouth. The moment they settled into place, a burst of laughter erupted from the room. The fake dentures were oversized and comically mismatched, giving Martha an endearing and hilarious appearance.

The room filled with laughter as Harold joined in, mimicking Martha's exaggerated smile. The residents couldn't help but be infected by the infectious joy, as smiles spread from face to face.

As the laughter subsided, Martha removed the fake dentures and returned them to Harold, her eyes brimming with gratitude. «Thank you, Harold, for reminding me that sometimes, the best way to face life's challenges is with a good laugh. You truly have a gift for brightening our days.»

From that day forward, the memory of Martha's misadventure with the mischievous dentures became a cherished tale in the retirement home. Laughter became their shared currency, and Harold continued to bring joy to the lives of his friends with his quick wit and playful antics.

The Whistle-Blowing Concert

In the picturesque town of Meadowbrook, nestled amidst rolling hills and blooming meadows, lived a group of lively seniors known for their zest for life and a love for music. Among them was Harold, a jovial gentleman with a mischievous twinkle in his eye and a passion for playing the harmonica.

One sunny afternoon, the community center buzzed with excitement as the residents gathered for a musical concert. Harold, eager to showcase his harmonica skills, took center stage, his instrument poised and ready.

As he began to play a lively tune, the room filled with the melodious notes of his harmonica. The audience, captivated by the sweet sounds, swayed along in their seats, tapping their feet to the rhythm.

But as Harold reached the crescendo of his performance, an unexpected twist unfolded. With a mischievous grin, he puckered his lips and let out a whistle that reverberated throughout the room. Startled, the audience burst into laughter, unable to contain their amusement at the unexpected addition to the concert.

The laughter only fueled Harold's mischievous spirit. He incorporated more whistles into his performance, each one perfectly timed to surprise and amuse his audience. The room echoed with laughter and applause, filling the air with an infectious joy.

Harold's whistling extravaganza turned the concert into a whimsical affair, uniting the community in laughter and delight. The residents marveled at Harold's unexpected talent and his ability to infuse the performance with an element of surprise.

As the concert came to a close, Harold took a bow amidst a standing ovation. Grinning from ear to ear, he felt a sense of accomplishment and fulfillment. His whistle-blowing antics had brought joy to the hearts of his fellow residents and proved that age was no barrier to playfulness and creativity.

From that day forward, the Meadowbrook community fondly referred to the concert as «The Whistle-Blowing Concert,» a cherished memory etched in their hearts. It reminded them that life was meant to be embraced with laughter, and that even the simplest acts of mischief could create moments of pure magic.

The story of «The Whistle-Blowing Concert» spread beyond Meadowbrook, inspiring others to embrace their inner mischievousness and find joy in unexpected ways. It served as a reminder that it's never too late to let loose, create smiles, and make beautiful music, even if it includes a few surprising whistles along the way.

The Forgiving Grandma

Have you ever witnessed an unexpected act of forgiveness? Let me share with you a heartwarming and funny story about a mischievous cat named Whiskers and her forgiving grandma.

Whiskers was a curious and playful cat who loved exploring every nook and cranny of her grandma's house. One sunny afternoon, while prancing around the living room, Whiskers accidentally knocked over a beautiful and cherished vase that belonged to her grandma.

The delicate vase shattered into countless pieces, causing a loud crash that echoed through the room. Whiskers froze in shock, her eyes wide with guilt. She knew she had done something wrong.

Just then, grandma entered the room, her eyes widening in surprise as she took in the scene. Instead of getting angry or upset, she simply sighed and knelt down to survey the mess. Whiskers nervously approached her, rubbing against her leg, seeking forgiveness.

With a smile on her face, grandma gently scooped up Whiskers in her arms and said, «Oh, my mischievous little Whiskers, accidents happen. It's just a vase, and what's more important is that you're safe.» Whiskers purred with relief, feeling the warmth of grandma's forgiveness. Grandma didn't hold onto anger or frustration but chose to see the love and joy that Whiskers brought into her life.

Together, they cleaned up the broken pieces, reminiscing about the memories that the vase held. Grandma shared stories of its origin, and Whiskers listened intently, snuggled in her lap.

From that day forward, Whiskers learned a valuable lesson about forgiveness. She became more cautious in her explorations but also knew that her grandma's love was unconditional. They formed an unbreakable bond based on trust and understanding.

In the years that followed, Whiskers continued to be mischievous, sometimes knocking over other items or climbing onto shelves she shouldn't have. But each time, grandma would simply chuckle, gently scold Whiskers, and shower her with love.

The story of Whiskers and her forgiving grandma reminds us of the power of forgiveness and unconditional love. It teaches us that mistakes happen, but it's how we respond to them that truly matters. By forgiving others, we create a space for healing and growth.

So, the next time you find yourself in a situation where forgiveness is needed, think of Whiskers and her grandma. Embrace the power of forgiveness, let go of grudges, and nurture the bonds that bring us joy and love.

The Hilarious Hide-and-Seek with Hank the Hound

In a quiet suburb, lived a jolly old man named Henry. He had a brilliant idea to entertain his friends who were living with dementia. He invited his neighbors and a dog named Hank for a hilarious game of hide-and-seek.

Everyone gathered at the park as Henry explained the rules of the game. Hank was a true pro at hide-and-seek, and they were all in for a delightful adventure.

Henry shouted, «Ready or not, here I come!» and everyone scattered. Hank, being an energetic and curious hound, dashed to the farthest corner of the park, preparing to hide.

One of the participants, an elderly lady named Martha, stumbled out of the bushes and accidentally stepped on Hank's tail. Startled, Hank mistook her for the seeker who had to catch him. Laughter erupted as they witnessed this unexpected chase.

Soon enough, Henry found Hank hiding behind a large tree. Hank got startled and darted off, sniffing everyone in his path. This sparked even more laughter as Hank unexpectedly sniffed each participant.

The game continued, and each time Hank found a new hiding spot, he playfully sniffed everyone, eliciting joyous laughter and delight from the participants.

His agility and enthusiasm infected everyone, even those living with dementia, and they actively took part in the game.

After the game, everyone gathered together to share their experiences. Smiles adorned their faces, and laughter filled the air. This simple game of hide-and-seek with Hank brought so much joy and laughter that they momentarily forgot their troubles and found moments of pure happiness.

In that moment, they realized that laughter had the power to unite, uplift spirits, and create cherished memories. Hank, with his playful spirit, became a beloved companion, bringing laughter and light to their lives.

And whenever they thought back to that day, they couldn't help but smile, knowing that the hilarious hide-and-seek with Hank had brightened their days and created a bond that would forever hold a special place in their hearts.

The Mischievous Parrot and the Stolen Breakfast

Once upon a time, in a cozy nursing home, there lived a mischievous parrot named Polly. Polly was known for his clever tricks and hilarious antics, bringing laughter and joy to all the residents. One morning, as the residents gathered for breakfast in the dining hall, a comical incident unfolded.

The aroma of freshly cooked pancakes filled the air, and the residents eagerly awaited their breakfast. But before the staff could distribute the plates, Polly swooped down from his perch and snatched a pancake right off a plate.

Everyone burst into laughter as Polly squawked with delight, proudly clutching the stolen pancake in his beak. He hopped from table to table, teasing the residents, who playfully tried to retrieve their breakfast from the crafty parrot.

Amidst the laughter and chaos, the staff tried to regain control, but Polly's antics were too amusing to interrupt. With each attempt to retrieve the pancake, Polly would swiftly dodge their hands and fly to a different table, leaving everyone in stitches.

Finally, one of the residents, an elderly gentleman named Mr. Jenkins, devised a plan. He held out a small piece of banana, enticing Polly with his favorite treat. The mischievous parrot couldn't resist the temptation and swooped down, dropping the pancake in exchange for the banana.

The room erupted in applause and laughter as Mr. Jenkins triumphantly reclaimed his pancake. Polly, now content with his banana treat, perched himself on Mr. Jenkins' shoulder, squawking with satisfaction.

From that day forward, Polly became the beloved breakfast companion at the nursing home. His thieving adventures brought laughter and lightheartedness to the residents' mornings, turning a simple meal into a delightful spectacle.

The incident with the stolen breakfast reminded everyone that life's little surprises and unexpected moments of laughter could brighten even the dullest of days. Polly, with his mischievous spirit, taught the residents the value of embracing joy and finding humor in the simplest of situations.

And so, in that cozy nursing home, the story of the mischievous parrot and the stolen breakfast became a legend, bringing smiles to the faces of residents for years to come. Polly's playful presence served as a reminder to cherish each moment, savor the laughter, and appreciate the joy that can be found in the most unexpected places.

The Whimsical Hat Collection

In a quaint village nestled amidst rolling hills, resided a lively and fashionable grandmother named Evelyn. Evelyn possessed an insatiable passion for fashion and her most treasured possession was her whimsical hat collection. Each hat was a unique masterpiece, adorned with feathers, ribbons, and exquisite details that reflected Evelyn's vibrant personality.

Every day, Evelyn carefully selected a hat to wear, each one telling a story or capturing a different mood. There was the wide-brimmed sun hat adorned with a cascade of colorful flowers, perfect for bright summer days. The elegant velvet hat with a delicate lace veil, reserved for special occasions. And the playful polka-dot cap she sported during family picnics, evoking laughter and delight.

Evelyn's grandchildren, Lily and Ethan, adored their fashionable grandma and often joined her in playful adventures centered around her hat collection. They would spend hours trying on different hats, giggling at their reflections in the mirror, and imagining the tales that each hat held.

One sunny afternoon, while arranging her hats on a display shelf, Evelyn discovered a tiny note peeking out from beneath one of them. Intrigued, she unfolded the note, revealing a message from Lily and Ethan. It read, «Dear Grandma, let's have a whimsical hat parade!»

Evelyn's eyes sparkled with excitement as she shared the idea with her grandchildren.

They dedicated days to prepare for the grand event, crafting invitations for friends and family, and selecting outfits that complemented their chosen hats.

The day of the whimsical hat parade arrived, and Evelyn's home transformed into a vibrant wonderland. The garden was adorned with colorful bunting, and a red carpet guided guests to the main stage. Music filled the air as Evelyn, Lily, and Ethan, donning their most extravagant hats, led the procession.

One by one, guests joined the parade, showcasing their own unique hat creations. Towering top hats adorned with miniature garden scenes, feathery fascinators with cascading ribbons, and even a hat fashioned to resemble a majestic peacock.

Laughter echoed through the streets as spectators marveled at the whimsical hats and their wearers. The parade evolved into a joyous celebration of self-expression and the enchantment of imagination. People from all walks of life, young and old, united to appreciate the artistry and spirit of the moment.

Evelyn beamed with pride as she watched her grandchildren, Lily and Ethan, confidently leading the way. The hat parade had not only brought the community together but also encouraged everyone to embrace their individuality and celebrate the beauty of self-expression.

From that day forward, the whimsical hat parade became an annual tradition in the village. Evelyn's collection expanded as friends and neighbors added their unique hats to the mix. It became a symbol of unity, creativity, and the sheer delight of embracing one's true self.

The Forgetful Duo

In a lively retirement community, two best friends, Martha and Harold, embarked on their daily adventures together. Despite their age, they approached life with a youthful spirit and an unwavering sense of humor. They were known as the dynamic duo, always ready for a good laugh and to brighten everyone's day.

One sunny morning, Martha woke up with a nagging feeling that she had forgotten something important. She confided in Harold, hoping he could help her piece together the puzzle. Harold, with a twinkle in his eye, reassured Martha that they would solve the mystery together.

They strolled through the vibrant streets, playfully jogging Martha's memory with random clues and hints. Laughter filled the air as they relished the joy of their friendship and the whimsical nature of their quest.

The community became their playground as they revisited familiar places that triggered memories. They stopped by the local bakery, where the aroma of freshly baked pastries filled the air. They even paid a visit to the park, where they had shared countless picnics under a giant oak tree.

Through their laughter-filled journey, Martha's forgotten memory began to unravel. With each passing moment, pieces of the puzzle fell into place. It wasn't the destination that mattered; it was the joy of the adventure and the shared moments of laughter and companionship.

And then, just as they were about to give up, Harold playfully exclaimed, «I remember! You left your favorite hat at the ice cream parlor!» Martha's face lit up with relief and amusement.

Hand in hand, they made their way to the ice cream parlor, where Martha's beloved hat awaited her. The staff greeted them with warm smiles and applause. It was a celebration of friendship, laughter, and the triumph of memory over forgetfulness.

From that day forward, Martha and Harold embraced their forgetful moments as opportunities for laughter and adventure. They became the resident comedians, inspiring others to embrace their own forgetful moments with grace and lightheartedness.

Their mischievous spirit and ability to find humor in every situation enriched their lives and the lives of others. Martha and Harold's friendship served as a shining example of resilience, joy, and the power of laughter to navigate the twists and turns of life.

And so, in that vibrant retirement community, Martha and Harold continued their journey hand in hand, creating laughter-filled memories that would be treasured for a lifetime. Their friendship reminded everyone that age is just a number, and with a lighthearted spirit and a good friend by your side, every day can be an adventure worth celebrating.

The Grand Pajama Party Revival

In the quiet suburban neighborhood of Maplewood, two spirited grandmothers, Alice and Margaret, reminisced about their carefree childhood days filled with laughter and mischief. Determined to relive the joy of their past, they planned a grand pajama party with their close-knit group of friends known as the «Golden Girls Gang.»

Together, they transformed Margaret's living room into a whimsical haven, adorned with vintage pajamas, fluffy slippers, and an array of sleeping caps. The room became a nostalgic tribute to their long-lost sleepovers, complete with fairy lights, streamers, and a mountain of plush pillows.

As the evening approached, excitement filled the air. The «Golden Girls Gang» arrived one by one, shedding their mature personas and embracing their inner children. Laughter and giggles echoed as they shared stories, danced to '50s tunes, and played lively rounds of «Truth or Dare,» rediscovering the carefree spirit of their youth.

Amidst the festivities, Alice surprised everyone with warm homemade cookies, evoking a wave of nostalgia and creating a sense of warmth and togetherness. The night became a journey back in time, reliving cherished memories and forging new ones, reminding them that age was just a number.

The grand pajama party became an annual tradition, cherished by Alice, Margaret, and the «Golden Girls Gang.»

With each passing year, they added new twists to the festivities, from karaoke sessions to impromptu fashion shows. Their enduring friendship inspired the entire neighborhood, proving that fun and embracing the inner child within knows no age limits.

Through laughter and camaraderie, the grandmothers brought a vibrant energy to their community, reminding everyone of the simple joys in life. The «Golden Girls Gang» became a symbol of unity, resilience, and the power of friendship.

As time went on, the grandmothers witnessed their children and grandchildren joining the tradition, passing down the legacy of the grand pajama party. The laughter, stories, and warm embraces created a tapestry of memories that bound their hearts together.

In the quiet neighborhood of Maplewood, the grand pajama party remained a cherished tradition, reminding everyone that age should never hinder having a good time. It served as a testament to the enduring spirit of friendship and the importance of embracing childlike wonder, regardless of age.

Grandpa's Zoo Adventure

Grandpa Henry, a sprightly octogenarian with a twinkle in his eye, embarked on a whimsical adventure to the local zoo. With his safari hat and trusty walking cane, he was determined to relive the magic of his childhood.

As he entered the zoo, Grandpa Henry was filled with joy at the vibrant sights and sounds of exotic animals. He walked with determination, determined to make this adventure unforgettable.

Grandpa Henry found himself standing before the towering giraffe enclosure. Feeling a connection with the graceful creatures, he playfully stretched his arms high, imitating their elongated necks. Onlookers burst into laughter, their smiles mirroring Grandpa's infectious spirit.

Eager for more fun, Grandpa Henry ventured to the monkey exhibit. He scratched his head and hopped from foot to foot, mimicking the mischievous antics of the swinging primates. The monkeys responded with playful chatter and dances, entertained by his lighthearted performance.

The zookeepers, captivated by Grandpa's exuberance, invited him to meet the resident parrots known for their mimicry. Grandpa engaged in a delightful conversation with the colorful birds, sharing stories and laughter.

As the day neared its end, Grandpa Henry found himself near the penguin habitat. Intrigued by their waddling walks, he joined their amusing procession.

With a twinkle in his eye, he shuffled alongside the penguins, his laughter harmonizing with their playful calls.

News of Grandpa Henry's unforgettable zoo adventure quickly spread. Visitors and zoo staff eagerly awaited his return, knowing his spirited presence would add magic to their day. He became a beloved fixture at the zoo, brightening the lives of animals and humans alike.

In the twilight of his zoo visits, Grandpa Henry reflected on the joy he had brought and received. The zoo had become his playground, a place where he embraced his inner child and reminded others to do the same. His adventurous spirit inspired visitors of all ages to cherish every moment and find delight in life's simplest pleasures.

Grandpa Henry's zoo adventure remained etched in the memories of those who witnessed his joyous escapades. His laughter echoed through the animal enclosures, creating a symphony of happiness long after he had departed.

For Grandpa Henry, the zoo had become a sanctuary where he discovered the eternal child within. In his vibrant spirit, the zoo would forever be a place of laughter, adventure, and the timeless magic of embracing life's wild and wonderful moments.

The Elusive Slipper: A Hilarious Quest for the Perfect Fit

In the quaint village of Willowbrook, a spirited grandmother named Beatrice was known for her vibrant personality and mischievous twinkle in her eye. With a particular weakness for shoes, she had a vast and colorful collection, but one type of shoe had eluded her—a perfect-fitting slipper.

One sunny afternoon, Beatrice entered a charming shoe boutique that had just opened in town. She admired the array of stylish footwear, and her eyes sparkled when she spotted a display of elegant slippers. Determined to find the one that would fit like a dream, she approached the salesperson with a mischievous smile.

«I'm on a mission to find the slipper that fits just right. Do you think you can help me?» Beatrice asked playfully.

Intrigued by Beatrice's enthusiasm, the salesperson happily obliged. They brought out an assortment of slippers, but none seemed to fit Beatrice's feet perfectly. Undeterred, Beatrice couldn't resist making a joke, exclaiming, «Well, it seems like my feet have developed a talent for staying one step ahead of the perfect slipper!»

The salesperson chuckled along, appreciating Beatrice's lighthearted approach. They continued their search, determined to find the slipper that would bring Beatrice the comfort she sought.

As the fitting process continued, the boutique became a scene of laughter and amusement. Beatrice tried on slippers of all shapes and sizes, playfully wiggling her toes and making humorous remarks. The salesperson joined in the banter, turning the shoe fitting into an entertaining event.

Their light-hearted exchanges spread joy to the other customers, who couldn't help but chuckle at the delightful spectacle unfolding before them.

After trying on numerous slippers, Beatrice finally found a pair that fit perfectly. They were vibrant and whimsical, adorned with shimmering sequins. As she slipped them on, a contented smile graced her face.

With a wink and a nod to the salesperson, Beatrice exclaimed, «Well, it looks like my feet have finally found their Cinderella moment! These slippers were worth the search and all the laughs along the way!»

The boutique erupted in laughter and applause. Beatrice's infectious humor and unwavering spirit had transformed a simple shopping experience into a cherished memory for everyone involved.

From that day forward, whenever Beatrice wore her perfect-fitting slippers, she couldn't help but smile, recalling the hilarious quest she had embarked upon to find them. Her mischievous spirit continued to inspire laughter and joy, reminding all who knew her that a sense of humor could turn even the most mundane moments into extraordinary adventures.

Tea and Masquerade: A Delightful Tradition

In the picturesque town of Willowbrook, two inseparable friends, Amelia and Sophia, embarked on a whimsical tradition that brought joy to their lives every Friday. Their shared love for tea and a touch of playfulness infused their friendship and sparked an idea.

Amelia had a mischievous glimmer in her eyes as she suggested, «What if we turn our peaceful tea gatherings into a weekly masquerade? Let's add a sprinkle of magic and mystery to our Fridays!» Excitement filled the air as they planned their first masquerade tea party. Vintage dresses, sparkling masks, and shimmering accessories were unearthed from trunks. Every week, they carefully selected their ensembles, eager to unveil their hidden personas and embrace the enchantment of the occasion.

On the inaugural Friday, the room was filled with the aroma of freshly brewed tea and the laughter of anticipation. Transformed by their elaborate costumes, Amelia and Sophia entered the enchanting space adorned with twinkling lights and colorful decorations.

Sipping tea from delicate porcelain cups, they shared secrets, dreams, and whimsical tales. The characters they portrayed added an extra layer of mystery and intrigue to their conversations, inviting them to explore new facets of their personalities and delve into the depths of their imaginations.

Amelia, dressed as a mischievous jester with a sparkling mask, entertained Sophia with witty jokes and lively antics. Sophia, adorned as an elegant enchantress with an ornate feathered mask, captivated Amelia with tales of enchantment and far-off lands. Together, they wove a vivid tapestry of whimsy and laughter.

The extraordinary masquerade tea parties soon became the talk of the town. Friends and neighbors joined in the festivities, and the tradition grew, weaving a web of camaraderie and celebration that transcended age and background.

Every Friday, the tea table transformed into a magical gathering where laughter echoed and dreams came to life. Masks created an air of delightful mystery, allowing everyone to step into a world where imagination reigned supreme.

As the years passed, Amelia and Sophia remained faithful to their tradition, cherishing the bonds they had formed and the memories they had created. The masquerade tea parties became a symbol of friendship, joy, and the indomitable spirit residing within their hearts.

The magic of the masquerade extended far beyond their teacup-filled room. It inspired them to embrace the wonders of life, don masks of courage during challenging times, and find reasons to celebrate even in the simplest moments.

Grandma's Tales: A Timeless Connection

As the sun bathed the cozy room in warm hues, Grandma Margaret sat in her favorite armchair at the nursing home, a glimmer of excitement in her eyes. Today was a special day - her beloved grandchildren were coming to visit. They had always been captivated by her stories, and she couldn't wait to share more tales from her vibrant past.

As the grandchildren arrived, their faces lit up with joy, eager to hear Grandma Margaret's enchanting stories. They gathered around her, leaning in with anticipation. With a smile that carried years of wisdom and adventure, Grandma began to recount the tales of her youth.

She took them on a journey through time, sharing tales of her mischievous childhood pranks, heartwarming family gatherings, and the lessons she learned along the way. With each story, her memories came alive, painting vivid pictures in the minds of her attentive grandchildren.

They marveled at Grandma Margaret's resilience and courage as she recounted her youthful adventures, from exploring hidden caves to participating in daring sports competitions. Her stories were filled with laughter, tears, and the triumphs of the human spirit. As the afternoon unfolded, the room buzzed with laughter and heartfelt conversations.

The grandchildren eagerly asked questions, wanting to know more about their family's history and the experiences that shaped Grandma Margaret into the person they admired so much.

Occasionally, Grandma Margaret would pause, her eyes sparkling with fondness as she shared anecdotes about their parents when they were young. These stories connected the generations, weaving a tapestry of love, resilience, and shared heritage.

Through her stories, Grandma Margaret transported her grandchildren to a bygone era, igniting their imagination and instilling a sense of pride in their family's legacy. They hung onto her every word, cherishing the intimate moments and life lessons woven into each tale.

As the day drew to a close, the grandchildren realized that Grandma Margaret's stories were not only about the past but also about the present. They realized the importance of embracing the moments and creating their own stories, just as Grandma had done throughout her life.

With grateful hearts, they bid Grandma Margaret farewell, knowing that her stories would forever be etched in their hearts. The connection they shared through those tales would remain a guiding light, reminding them of the wisdom, strength, and love that flowed through their family's veins.

The Jolly Jest Fest

In the lively town of Gigglesville, known for its boisterous humor and love for all things funny, there lived a man named Chuck, the crowned king of American wit. With his quick one-liners and impeccable comedic timing, Chuck was the life of every party and the source of endless laughter.

One sunny day, Chuck embarked on an outrageous adventure that would test his comedic prowess. Armed with his trusty rubber chicken and a truckload of puns, he set out to bring laughter to the far corners of the country.

Hitching a ride with a lanky cowboy named Tex in a beat-up pick-up truck, the two immediately hit it off with their shared love for good-natured banter. Chuck boldly declared, «Tex, I bet I can make you laugh so hard you'll forget how to wrangle cattle!»

Tex chuckled and replied, «Well, partner, I reckon you'll have to bring your A-game if you wanna outwit this old cowboy!»

Their journey took them through small towns and big cities alike, and Chuck seized every opportunity to unleash his brand of American humor. At a roadside diner, he cracked a joke to the waitress, saying, «Hey, I asked for a quick meal, not a slow-motion reenactment of Thanksgiving!»

The patrons erupted into laughter, and even the stern-faced cook couldn't help but crack a smile. Chuck's infectious humor transformed the diner into a jovial comedy club.

As their adventure continued, Chuck and Tex stumbled upon a county fair hosting a stand-up comedy contest. Chuck couldn't resist the challenge and took the stage, armed with his rubber chicken and a pocketful of zingers.

With each joke and pun, Chuck had the audience rolling in the aisles. He quipped, «Why did the scarecrow win an award? Because he was outstanding in his field!» The crowd erupted into fits of laughter, and Chuck walked away with the coveted comedy crown, his rubber chicken held high in triumph.

Their laughter-filled journey also led them to a bustling comedy club in the heart of the city. Chuck stepped onto the stage, facing a diverse audience eager for a dose of American humor. He unleashed a routine that blended observational comedy with hilarious anecdotes, poking fun at everyday quirks and cultural nuances.

As the crowd roared with laughter, Chuck felt a deep sense of fulfillment. He had united people from all walks of life through the power of laughter, proving that humor transcends boundaries and brings people together.

Word of Chuck's uproarious adventures spread like wildfire, attracting comedy enthusiasts from far and wide to witness his comedic genius. From dive bars to late-night TV shows, Chuck's jokes became legendary, leaving audiences in stitches and earning him the title of America's Funniest Jester. As Chuck and Tex reached their final destination, they looked back on their uproarious journey with hearts full of joy. They had succeeded in spreading the infectious spirit of American humor, leaving a trail of laughter in their wake.

Grandpa Chef: A Flavorful Tale

Once upon a time, in a small village nestled amidst rolling hills, there lived a jolly old grandfather named Henry. He was known far and wide for his remarkable culinary skills and his insatiable love for food. Henry's kitchen was his sanctuary, and he delighted in preparing mouthwatering feasts for his family and friends.

One day, Henry stumbled upon an old recipe book hidden away in his attic. Its pages were filled with secret family recipes passed down through generations. Intrigued, he decided to recreate one of the dishes—a magical recipe for golden apple pie.

As Henry mixed the ingredients with care, a peculiar thing happened. With each stir of the spoon, a sweet aroma filled the air, and the apples began to dance in the pan. Henry's eyes widened in disbelief as he witnessed this extraordinary sight. The apples twirled and waltzed, forming a delightful spectacle of flavors and colors.

Word of Henry's dancing apple pie spread like wildfire throughout the village. People flocked to his humble abode, eager to witness this edible ballet. They marveled at the enchanting display and savored every delicious bite, their taste buds tingling with delight.

Henry's fame as the «Dancing Grandpa Chef» grew, and soon, he found himself performing at grand culinary events.

His kitchen became a stage, and his dishes became captivating performances that left the audience in awe.

But amidst the applause and accolades, Henry remained humble. He knew that the true magic was not in the dancing apples, but in the joy and love he infused into his cooking. It was the laughter and togetherness that filled his home whenever he shared a meal with his loved ones.

And so, Henry continued to cook with passion and spread happiness through his delectable creations. His kitchen remained a place of warmth and laughter, where friends and family gathered to savor the flavors of his culinary masterpieces.

To this day, the tale of Henry, the Dancing Grandpa Chef, lives on in the hearts of those who were fortunate enough to experience his enchanting dishes. And the dancing apple pie remains a symbol of the magic that can be found in the simplest pleasures—good food, laughter, and the love that binds us all together.

The Silver Squad's Spectacular Scavenger Hunt

In the lively town of Culinary Haven, a group of spirited seniors known as the Grand Squad embarked on a mouthwatering adventure. With a shared passion for food and a zest for life, they set out on a gastronomic expedition like no other.

Led by their indomitable leader, Grandma Grace, the Grand Squad explored the town's hidden culinary gems, from charming cafes to bustling markets. Armed with empty stomachs and a curiosity for new flavors, they indulged in delectable treats and savored every bite.

Their expedition took them on a whirlwind tour of diverse cuisines and culinary traditions. They sampled spicy street food, delicate pastries, and hearty homemade dishes, each bite awakening their taste buds and igniting their senses.

With each new meal, the Grand Squad discovered not only the delights of the local cuisine but also the stories behind the recipes and the people who prepared them. They learned the importance of preserving culinary traditions and sharing the love of food with others.

As their adventure unfolded, the Grand Squad bonded over shared meals and laughter-filled conversations. They traded recipes, swapped cooking tips, and reveled in the joy of discovering new flavors together.

The love for food brought them closer, creating a tapestry of friendship and delicious memories.

Word of their epic gastronomic journey spread throughout the town, inspiring others to embark on their culinary expeditions. The Grand Squad became local celebrities, beloved for their adventurous spirits and contagious passion for food.

And so, as the Grand Squad reached the end of their gastronomic expedition, their hearts were filled with gratitude and contentment. They had not only satisfied their appetites but also nourished their souls with the joy of exploration and the bonds of friendship.

In the town of Culinary Haven, the Grand Squad's gastronomic expedition became a legendary tale, reminding everyone of the transformative power of food and the endless possibilities that await those who dare to explore the culinary world.

So, grab your forks and join the Grand Squad on their next gastronomic adventure. Let your taste buds be tantalized, your hearts be filled with joy, and your love for food be reignited as you savor the flavors of life alongside these spirited seniors.

Dancing Duo: Laughter Unleashed

Once upon a time in the whimsical town of Wackyville, there lived a quirky penguin named Percy. Percy had a peculiar talent – he could dance like nobody's business! His fancy footwork brought joy to everyone he met.

One sunny day, Percy decided to put on a dance performance in the town square. As he twirled and spun, the townspeople couldn't help but laugh and cheer. But Percy's dancing drew the attention of a grumpy old cat named Mr. Whiskers.

Unable to resist the rhythm, Mr. Whiskers joined in, attempting his own dance moves. The result was a hilarious spectacle as he stumbled and wiggled. The crowd erupted in laughter, and even Percy couldn't keep a straight face.

In that moment, Percy realized that laughter and kindness could bridge any divide. From that day forward, Percy and Mr. Whiskers became the town's dynamic dancing duo, spreading joy and merriment wherever they went.

Their adventures taught the townspeople that even the most unlikely friendships can blossom when we embrace humor and let kindness guide our steps. And so, in Wackyville, laughter became the soundtrack of their lives, reminding them to dance through life with a smile and an open heart.

CONCLUSION

As we come to the end of this book, we'd like to share a few thoughts. These stories about the old folks are not just amusing and entertaining, but they also carry a profound message. They remind us of the value of every moment, the power of friendship and love, and that age should never be a barrier to living life to the fullest.

In these tales, we've encountered unique characters – grandpas and grandmas full of life experience and wisdom. We've witnessed how they perceive the world with humor and optimism, how their hearts fill with joy and inspiration. They show us that old age is a time of possibilities, a time when we can continue to dream, learn, and share our wisdom with others.

Each story in this book serves as a reminder that laughter is the best medicine, that friendship and support help us overcome challenges, and that it's important to maintain our playfulness and openness to new adventures even in our golden years.

We hope that these stories leave a lasting impression in your hearts, reminding you of the value of every moment and our capacity to find joy and share laughter.

Thank you for joining us in these lighthearted tales of the old folks. We hope they leave you with a sense of joy, laughter, and hope for a brighter future. Until we meet again!

Martin Miller

Made in the USA
Las Vegas, NV
23 November 2024

12512837R00087